FORREST H. PATTON

The Psychology of Closing Sales

A SPECTRUM BOOK

Prentice-Hall, Inc., Englewood Cliffs, N.J. 07632

Library of Congress Cataloging in Publication Data

PATTON, FORREST H.
The psychology of closing sales.

"A Spectrum Book."
Includes index.
1. Selling—Psychological aspects. I. Title.
HF5438.8.P75P37 1984   658.8'5   84-9835
ISBN 0-13-735671-4
ISBN 0-13-735663-3 (pbk.)

To my father, David C. Patton, an exceptional
sales engineer, who practiced complete integrity
throughout the selling process.

This book is available at a special discount when ordered
in bulk quantities. Contact Prentice-Hall, Inc., General
Publishing Division, Special Sales, Englewood Cliffs, N. J. 07632.

A SPECTRUM BOOK

Manufacturing buyer: Doreen Cavallo
Cover design © 1984 by Jeannette Jacobs

ISBN 0-13-735671-4

ISBN 0-13-735663-3 {PBK.}

1   2   3   4   5   6   7   8   9   10

Printed in the United States of America

Prentice-Hall International, Inc., London
Prentice-Hall of Australia Pty. Limited, Sydney
Prentice-Hall Canada Inc., Toronto
Prentice-Hall of India Private Limited, New Delhi
Prentice-Hall of Japan, Inc., Tokyo
Prentice-Hall of Southeast Asia Pte. Ltd., Singapore
Whitehall Books Limited, Wellington, New Zealand
Editora Prentice-Hall do Brasil Ltda., Rio de Janeiro

Contents

Preface

This book is about being *exceptional* in closing sales—not just very good . . . but exceptional. That difference between being very good and being exceptional is small . . . perhaps 5 percent. In any profession you will find this "winning edge." You will find many who are very good—and then there are the exceptional few who, though only a fraction better, are making twice or maybe 10 times as much in income.

This book will take you, step by step, through the elements of persuasion and closing sales effectively. Those of you who are experienced in selling will see *why* certain things you do work so well. But, more importantly, you will gather fresh, new concepts and advanced psychological strategies in today's *consultive sell* approach. For you who are new to selling, it will save you many, many frustrating years of trial and error as you leap ahead by reading and rereading these chapters.

Closing a sale starts with the first emotional impression you make on the phone or in person. Much of closing is *feeling* and *sensing* the right thing to do at a given moment along the way. I have taken these psychological actions and reactions and set them down as "how to" methods.

In preparation I have interviewed hundreds of key decision makers: what they liked and disliked about salespeople's approach and closing; how salespeople persuaded them to change suppliers; how salespeople overcame their objections and closed; how salespeople got through to them on the phone or in person without stepping on a "screen's" toes. This was all measured against my own years of selling experience and the experience of many of the very top people in selling today.

Straight-forward, high-type professional selling is a most rewarding career. Being exceptional in this career is simply *finding out the right things to do . . . and then doing those things consistently!* In these pages you will not find generalities or platitudes. Every bit of it is specific and realistic method. It is a track to run on . . . a track that will carry you through real-life selling in getting the sophisticated decision maker of today to buy your ideas, your products, and your services.

1
Bold Is Beautiful

This book digs deeply into the psychology of closing sales. It is only the exceptional person who has the desire to explore these depths; the book aims at that exceptional person. This is the person who wants and fully expects to be outstanding. Selling is a *demanding* occupation: It is demanding physically, mentally, and emotionally.

These demands require that you use psychology—not just on others, but on yourself as well. You *must* use it on yourself first. You must use psychology on yourself if you hope to develop a selling attitude—an attitude that starts with boldness!

Right now I'd like you to think of yourself as bold—not obnoxious . . . not reckless . . . just plain bold. Be bold in thinking, bold in desires, bold in planning, and bold in your actions. Selling means closing, and to close the big ones, the tough ones, you must take risks. That's where boldness comes in. When you are bold, you extend yourself; you are willing to become vulnerable.

If you always play it safe in life, you will get by but you will never feel that you've really lived. As the years go by you'll be haunted by feelings that it could have been different. You will feel a kind of creeping dissatisfaction with your life as annoying thoughts come bubbling to the surface. And as this "still, small voice" presses its way to the forefront of your consciousness, you may hear it say, "I could have done it . . . if only I hadn't doubted . . . why didn't I have the courage to try . . . if only I hadn't been so concerned over what others might think . . . if only I had listened to me. . . ." There will always be somebody who can tell you why you can't close the "big ones."

Bold is beautiful. Begin this new practice of boldness at once. Put out of your mind any doubts you have about yourself. I don't care if you've been in sales for 30 years or for 30 minutes. Of course, you will never get rid of *every* self-doubt; nobody does that. But you *can* derail these doubts as they come rolling through your mind. You can decide to go with *boldness* instead. Grab hold of this idea, starting today . . . this very moment. Don't just resolve to do it, start as you are reading this. I promise that it will make such a difference in your selling productivity—and in your life! And even if you feel some satisfaction with your "boldness level" right now, try *extending it* and see what happens.

As a football player once put it, "You're going to be 'hit' on some plays you make. Every big play is not a winner. But you learn to get up off the grass and go for the next one."

BUILD BOLDNESS
BY ASKING FOR LARGER ORDERS

Start this day to ask for *big* orders instead of grabbing the small, easy ones. Suggest the higher-priced items.

Most salespeople find themselves "selling short" on routine sales calls. Fear enters the scene; maybe we hesitate recommending the larger quantity or higher price for fear of a turndown. "Selling short" can become a tough habit to shake. If you feel that you have this tendency—this reflex for quickly talking lower prices or smaller quantities—here's what you can do to break the habit. Starting with your next call, first make the call *mentally*. In your mind, hear yourself asking for the larger order. Then do it for real as boldness takes over. Sure, you will feel a little anxiety at first, but that's perfectly normal. Suddenly, it will happen. You won't ask for too many of those big ones before somebody says "Yes!" And you will feel elated, for you will have taken a giant leap forward.

YOUR BEST PROSPECTS
MAY BE YOUR PRESENT CUSTOMERS

Take a close look at your present customers. What are the possibilities for increased business? How about that good account that you've been getting fair-sized orders from, but whom you've never really pushed for larger volume? One day you could walk in and find that a competitor has just beat you out with an order for five times your usual volume.

Bill Robinson, a printing salesman, had gotten into the habit of "grabbing the order and running." Most of Bill's *regular* customers were usually ready to give him some kind of order when he called. He just took what they gave him. Then one day something happened that made him realize that he was just "taking orders" instead of selling.

> I had called on this customer, and I happened to notice that some of the merchandise on the floor had new "trade name" decals on them—decals that I sometimes sold. I asked about them. My customer said, "I didn't know you sold decals. I thought you just took orders for printing!" Now that really hurt. Then it hit me. I was limiting myself by not trying to sell the full line on every call.

Never Assume a Buyer's Budget Limits

How do you know what a potential customer can afford? A friend of mine sold NC systems—computerized control systems for large industrial machinery. One of his electronics customers had been gradually building onto the system to include more and more of the punch presses in the plant. Only once did this salesman mention to the customer that all the lathes and mills should also be included. The response he got was they just didn't have it in the budget . . . that the word "upstairs" was that they wouldn't be making any capital expenditures for some time.

Two months later a competitor came in with a specific plan showing how the controls on the lathes and mills would pay for themselves in just 10 months. That competitor walked out with a very large order covering all the mills and lathes in the plant. It taught my friend an expensive lesson: Don't wait for your competitor to find out what your client can afford. Find out for yourself by asking for the business. *Be bold. Ask!*

TO BE EXCEPTIONAL, YOU MUST TAKE RISKS

Most people play it safe. Most people settle for being average. To be an exceptional closer, you simply *must* take risks. I'm not talking about being foolhardy, unthinking, or reckless. I'm talking about taking calculated risks to be an outstanding closer. You must go after the large order, the big account. You must target the final decision maker and do everything possible to get to that person, yet keep the goodwill of any people who are acting as "screens" between you and the decision maker.

You must risk being different. An excellent salesman I know landed a long-term order with a large meat packer. This salesman sold for a radio station that had only fair listener numbers. The top buyer was coming to town to place budgets with a few select radio stations. They were going to do this by having each station representative present his or her story to the buyer in a hotel room. Every 30 minutes the buyer would listen to the pitch of a different rep. My friend realized that he didn't have a chance in this kind of comparative buying and would need to present his story in a unique style. He bought a woman's purse at Sears and put a typed note inside which said:

> We have a big female audience in the 21- to 49-age bracket. Seventy percent of our audience is female . . . they buy meat products, and we'd like to tell them about your fine meats.

Then he had the purse with the message sent into the hotel room by a bellman.

The buyer thought it was the most unique presentation he had ever seen. He bought. My friend had dared to be different.

There was, of course, a risk in this presentation. The buyer might have been offended at getting a purse . . . or maybe he wouldn't have liked the deviation from the personal presentation. It was a calculated risk, and it paid off.

A salesman in Tampa dared to be different. He sold large permanent signs, the kind you see in front of Kentucky Fried Chicken or McDonalds. In his case "being different" was working for a small sign company and having the nerve to tackle a prospect who used hundreds of huge, permanent, expensive signs nationwide. His persistence and boldness got him an interview with the company president. This president was probably amused that this representative from a tiny sign company thought he could compete with the large supplier that his company had used for years.

After the first call and turndown, the salesman didn't give up, however. He called again, and again. About a week after his third call, the salesman got a call from the company president. The regular supplier had blundered by failing to erect a sign in time for a grand opening of one of the stores. This salesman got a large sign order, and the little sign company he works for isn't little anymore.

What, really, are the "risks" in being bold? You're not going to get shot. No one is going to physically harm you. If you're turned down, it's simply your proposition that is not being accepted for the moment. So what are the *real* risks in being bold?

Boldness carries with it the risk that you will be exceptional! This means that you may have to risk being a loner. It means that you won't run with the flock. You won't have time to sit around the office making small talk . . . and you won't have time to do that with clients, either. You won't have time for those drop-in "conversation" calls. This doesn't mean that you'll be less pleasant, cooperative, or helpful; you simply won't be able to afford to *waste* time. And you'll need more time for yourself—more time for reflection, for ideas, for plans. And it may mean that you will have to take lunch with clients instead of cohorts.

Diana Smith is a sales presentative for Jim Stephenson & Associates, in Houston. She calls on architects and building engineers to convince them that they should specify the building hardware sold by her company. She has learned how to turn the lunch break into a real selling tool.

> Clients sometimes *expect* you to buy lunch. I don't object to this, but the way I do it, I get some real "mileage" out of it. I bring lunch in! What I'm talking about is a brown bag lunch. I'll call on a client and ask him to get all those key people together who would be working with my product. I'll bring in maybe a couple of buckets of fried chicken and a cooler of Cokes. Now I have a captive audience that I can make a slide presentation to.

Diana has learned to be different in a way that really impresses her clients. Do the job differently and your clients will perceive that you are different.

You risk stress when you step out in a bold and different way. No question about it. And there is high stress in going for the big orders and closing the tough ones. Selling is one of the most stressful occupations. A lot has been written about *avoiding* stress, but studies show that many people need *some* stress. In fact, there are people who seem to *thrive* on stress! My feeling is that if you're now in selling or thinking about getting into it, you require a good measure of stress in your life to function at your best.

BEATING THE FEAR
OF REJECTION

One of the most stressful situations beginning salespeople face is the flat turndown. It's not all that easy to keep your proposition separate from yourself and your ego. But you must do that; you must learn that it is not *you* that is being turned down—it is *only the proposal*! Rejection is *not* personal.

There are many facets of the selling process that may serve to blunt your high resolve to be bold. One is a habit of taking a turndown as a personal affront. What a shame and mistake that is! It can't be said often enough: It is not one's *self* that is being turned down; it is only the proposition.

The fear of rejection is one of the greatest obstacles to a willingness to make new prospect calls. To protect your ego, you may play little games with yourself when faced with the decision to make new calls. Here are a few psychological tricks that your mind might play on you.

1. Something on your desk needs to be taken care of. By now it's getting close to lunchtime. Better not try to make a call now. *There will always be things on your desk* that need attention. This is probably the greatest excuse in the world; it is guaranteed to keep you from being "rejected," keep you from being hurt.

2. You need to service some of your regular accounts. Frequent service calls leave little or no time for new prospect calls. In your heart you *know* you're overservicing, but you convince yourself that "staying in close touch" is a good idea. This is another way of burying your head in the sand . . . believing that you're working, and thus justifying the fact that you're not making new calls (and getting rejected).

3. On a new call you settle for making a presentation to a "screen" instead of trying to go higher where the final decision is made.

4. Personal business. You talk yourself into believing that it is urgent that you make several personal telephone calls. And it's easy to jump from this to taking time for an extra cup of coffee, or chatting with someone in the office. Perhaps you get the feeling that it's a bad time to make calls since people will be opening their mail this early in the morning. Maybe you'll just wait until afternoon (when it will be too late). Or maybe it's Friday—nobody is in the mood for business on Friday. Neat excuses. Any one of them is guaranteed to keep you from making those new calls and maybe being rejected.

Burn this into your brain: *You will not be turned down.* Maybe your presentation will, but that's not the same thing. We're all hungry for approval, and sometimes we get a turndown confused with feelings that the prospect doesn't approve of us. You must absolutely forget about your ego and "getting hurt" in selling. Instead, concern yourself with your expert product and service knowledge, and how you can tie this into the wants and problems of the prospect.

Certainly we want to please the prospect. But that approval should not be at the expense of letting the prospect "sell us" off our proposition. Preoccupation with approval can make a salesperson stop pressing for a close. You *must* adroitly press your case in the face of an entire series of "no's." Your purpose is to show the prospect certain benefits, not to gain approval. Fear of disapproval can cause you to quit in the face of mild prospect reluctance. You're not there just to show your prospect what a nice person you are, you're there to sell.

COMMIT YOURSELF TO BOLDNESS IN SELLING AND CLOSING

You must resolutely commit yourself to boldness in selling and in closing. Do that right now, this minute. Make a commitment to yourself. Your mind is the grandest of computers, so program it. Affirm for 30 days straight:

> Today I am bold, honest, and straightforward in all my thinking and all my plans. I help people with what I have to offer. Therefore, I close sales boldly and easily.

Say this to yourself each morning. Don't miss a single day. You're trying to chart this into the subconscious . . . program it into habit.

This isn't new; exceptional people in all walks of life have long been doing variations of this type of self-conditioning. Top athletes psyche themselves up constantly. Instead of "closing," they call it "winning." Just remember, when you "lose," it doesn't mean that your programming hasn't worked. This kind of mind programming *does* work. Winners all lose some battles on the way. Top closers take a turndown and go back for more. Every one of them has known defeat. They learn from every experience. But there are no excuses, no self-pitying. And remember, it's more fun to be exceptional! Resolve, now, to follow the exhortation of Goethe:

> *Whatever you can do, or dream you can, begin it! Boldness has genius, power and magic in it.*

2
Anatomy of Persuasion

You are into the close with your very first words, whether you are face-to-face with your prospect or talking over the telephone. Your prospect's computer brain is taking you in, clickity-click, clickity-click. You're being measured against your prospect's own emotional needs and wants. But the prospect is hardly aware of this quick evaluation. It is almost automatic. You help to satisfy the emotional cravings of the prospect—to that extent you are liked. And people usually buy from people they like.

PERSUASION KEY #1: YOU COME ACROSS AS A WORTHY PERSON

We like to do business with people who are sincere, warm, intelligent, knowledgeable, and confident.

Persuasion begins with the way you say your name. You may be a rapid talker, but however fast you are in delivering your sales message, let me urge you to be slow and careful about your name. Don't mumble or slur your name; don't let your first name blend into your last name. Put "space" between the two names when you say them aloud.

Your name is your "trademark," and you must take care that

your prospect hears it correctly. If you can think of any kind of mnemonic device to help in remembering your name, you should mention it when introducing yourself.

Be just as careful with the name of your company. Enunciate it carefully. Give your prospect's mind a chance to absorb all this new information. When you do this, you come across as worthy, as a winner.

PERSUASION KEY #2:
YOU LIFT THE PROSPECT'S EGO

There is a desperate need in all of us: It is crying out for satisfaction. We all want to feel important and deep inside we need to feel that we are smart, have a good heritage, and that we're attractive to the opposite sex. In short, we want to feel good about ourselves.

The Ego Is Like an Egg

The "egg" can crack, oh so easily! A kick in the shin hurts, but not nearly so much as a kick in the ego. That *really* hurts! So we need to protect the ego carefully. Since we want to feel good about ourselves, we don't want to hear or see anything that would make us feel *less* about ourselves.

This need to feel good about ourselves makes it difficult for us to openly accept criticism. This is why we can't stand "nit pickers." For example, you're riding in your car with someone. You're driving and your passenger says rather sharply, "Why did you turn there?" The tone in which the question is asked makes the question sound like a put-down. You can almost hear the word "dummy" after the question. How fragile is the shell of the egg that surrounds our ego!

Remember, your prospect has such a tender ego, too—he wants to feel smart, too. Deep in the recesses of the subconscious mind there may be doubts, however. Maybe there lurks a memory of a flunked course in school, of classmates getting high grades for the same course. Don't be mislead by the "adult," poised appearance of the person in front of you. Countless self-doubts plague us all.

There are many ways that you, as a sales pro, can give your prospect a lift and intensify any person's feeling of self-worth. When you give people this kind of "lift," they will usually want to hear more of what you have to say; they are much more receptive to your presentation. One sales trainer put it this way:

> When you give people what *they* want, they are motivated to give *you* what you want.

You have set a favorable stage for the sale. Before we get into the "how to do it" part, lets get clear about this. Selling through the use of psychology is *not manipulation*. A healthy personality can spot a phony. If what you're doing is trying to ingratiate yourself, forget it. Nobody likes fawning; most people can spot flattery. Even if they temporarily like it, they won't respect you for it.

Develop sincere feelings toward your clients. I'm talking about a genuine caring for your prospect or client as a person.

Lift Them With Your Dialogue

A first meeting might go something like this: "Miss Jones, I didn't realize that you had such a large operation as this." That's an oblique compliment, but it's really saying, "Hey, you're smart." For it to work, though, it would have to be something you really felt. Otherwise, it might sound like "I didn't think you were that smart."

Suppose you had previously met two of the client's employees and you commented on this meeting to your client. You might say something like, "I had a meeting with Mr. Rhineholz and Mr. Sawyer. They're very knowledgeable. You certainly have some fine people." That's like saying, "You're sharp, you know how to hire good people." Again, that would have to be a sincerely-felt comment to be effective.

Unless there is something that strikes you as very impressive, I'd suggest staying away from trophies, pictures, or ornaments on the client's desk . . . at least on the first call. This may seem too ingratiating. However, if it is really sincere—if the item really strikes you—there's nothing wrong with a remark. The real key is genuineness and spontaneity.

An illustration might help to clarify this point. I was conducting an advanced sales seminar when a salesman of considerable experience made this comment:

> My biggest problem is in selling to women. I have trouble on the first call. When I sit down, I try to find something I can make a nice remark about. It could be a picture of her daughter, or something like that. Many female prospects get tight-lipped and cool at this point. Men don't do that with me.

Several women in the group were quick to spot the answer. "You're patronizing," one of them said. "Men do that all the time and women resent it. Men think all they have to do is to say something nice and we'll fall into their laps and buy whatever they want us to. It's so phony!"

This particular salesman had been trained to "break the ice" when he first walks in, by looking for something to "say something nice about."

Your Body Language
Can Give Your Prospect a Lift

When you face your prospect, you are saying, "You are important to me." Have you noticed that at meetings and at parties, some people won't face you? They remain at an angle to you, and may even keep glancing around. Do you get the feeling that they are checking to see if perhaps there is someone more important around?

When you face your prospects, here is the sort of thing that is going through their minds:

"I like you because you give me pupil contact." Pupil contact also says "You're important to me." Many people give others a sort of hazy look that takes in the eyes. But pupil contact is holding the gaze for at least a few seconds, then taking in the eyes, then the face. I'm not talking about intimidation or staring someone down.

"I like you because you smile." What a persuasive tool! Yet many salespeople use it so sparingly. The trouble is, they don't really think about it—they don't develop the habit. Yet, it can pave the way right into the close. It can dissolve a prospect's anxieties at the moment of commitment. A smile says, "I care. I like you. I think you're important!"

PERSUASION KEY #3:
GIVE THEM WHAT THEY WANT

Give people what they want, and they will give you what you want. But what do people want? What do prospects want? Well, we all want many of the same things. Basically, we want the approval of others. We want love. We want to be recognized as worthy. We want security. We want good health. We want the necessities of life. And, of course, we want to feel good about ourselves. But let's get specific, and break this down further. Let's see how we can give a prospect what he or she wants. Some of these specifics could be such things as a desire for power, a need to be admired, the need to have what money can buy, the desire to look younger, look slimmer, to feel more energetic, the need for recognition or fame, for approval of friends and acquaintances.

Perhaps there is a strong desire for freedom. Most of us want to be attractive to the opposite sex, and need sexual activity, understanding, freedom from worry and anxiety, and a feeling of prestige. The list could go on ad infinitum.

All of us are on a daily search to satisfy our many wants and needs—and so are our prospects. When you, as a salesperson, help to satisfy any of these wants and needs, you persuade. And it all starts with caring.

You care enough to be considerate and you have the sense to know when your client is busy. You can also tell when there is a need to talk and you have the empathy to sense when a prospect is troubled. When you care, you remember special things about your prospect's or client's interests. If you come across an item of interest in the newspaper, you'll tear it out and send it to your client. You go out of your way to help without making a big deal out of it.

When You Care,
You *Really* Listen

This may well be the most powerful factor in the skill of persuasion. A good listener is rare. Too often, poor listeners aren't able to hide the fact that they aren't really listening, but only pretending to listen. What they're really doing is thinking about what they are going to say at the first opening in the conversation. When you really listen attentively, you give your client a decided lift, create a warm bond between the two of you, and engender genuine rapport. When you listen, you also help to satisfy the universal need for understanding. Sometimes a client will simply want to talk to someone about a problem, or just relate something that has happened to him or her.

Many of us, in this geared-up, computerized age, are finding far too little time for normal, relaxed interaction with others. Often it's difficult to find someone with the time and inclination to listen while we "unload." And, with both spouses working, it has gotten more difficult to really unload, even at home. There was a time when we thought that a sales pro had to dominate the sales interview by talking. Not anymore. If you're a really effective salesperson, you're a good listener—you've learned what a powerful, persuasive tool listening can be.

Robert Conklin, in his book, *How To Get People To Do Things*, points out some interesting facts regarding our fuller understanding of the sales rep's role. In one six-month study, he found that the lowest 10 percent of one salesforce talked an average of 30 minutes per presentation. By contrast, the top 10 percent talked an average of only 12 minutes per presentation!

Listening Can Lead
Right to the Order

I remember a call I made with a printing supply salesman. He was anxious to crack this particular account—a large user of printing. The salesman had made two prior calls that were nonproductive. This time, the prospect came out into the lobby and said, "Jim, I'm pretty jammed up. All I've got is a few minutes." Jim said, "That's OK . . . I've got something I want to show you . . . it won't take long."

As we walked back to the prospect's office, he continued to talk about how busy he was . . . trying to catch up after his trip to Israel. Jim said, "I didn't know you were going to Israel. I've never been there. Did you like it?"

"It was great," was the response. "We had a funny experience in Jerusalem. My daughter Ann got separated from us while we were shopping. Ann's just 16, but she's cool, and she didn't panic . . ." He continued to chat for about 25 minutes. My salesman friend was a study in rapt attention; he listened with total, concentrated interest. Suddenly, the prospect realized what time it was and jumped up.

"My gosh," he said, "Look, Jim . . . ah . . . I've just got to clear out some of this paperwork here. Look, we've got a 60,000-piece mail-out. Four colors, accordian fold, heavy stock. Schedule is set for 90 days from now. Bring a quote by Thursday . . . it'll be on 8½ by 11. Quote us on various weights. I think we can do some business."

All Jim had done was really listen. How many people really listen to us with concerned attention? Not many. Jim got the order. And I've since learned that he now has his own printing business.

When You Care,
Clients Feel Secure with You

Buyers worry—they want to feel secure about the purchase. Company presidents worry—they hope that stockholders and board members will approve of their decisions. Everybody wants to feel secure about his buying record. When the sales pro adds to that feeling of security, he or she adds to the persuasive force of a presentation.

In selling, you must be keenly aware of these emotional needs. We can sense these needs, because they also reside within our own psyche. You can identify these needs in someone else by observing certain mannerisms. Sometimes you will see it in a look, or in the way a person touches your product. You may hear it in certain voice inflections, or see it in certain ponderings and in the expressiveness of a pair of eyes.

You will learn to watch the way a prospect sits or stands. The more we try to understand a person's emotional needs and wants, the closer we come to the real essence of persuasion.

PERSUASION KEY #4:
THE POWER OF ENTHUSIASM

Enthusiasm isn't just waving the arms about. In fact, enthusiasm can be very quiet. It may be expressed in facial expressions, in manner, in the voice, in the eyes, and in the way one walks. Enthusiasm comes from 1) pride in oneself; 2) pride in one's company; and 3) pride in one's product or service.

One way to maintain high enthusiasm is to have a "pump up" session with a group of your sales colleagues about four times a year. Each salesperson brings a customer list to the meeting. One person acts as moderator while each salesperson explains why the customer bought, or why the customer is still with the company. Out of 20 or 30 of these stories will come some excellent testimonial stories which can be used by everyone in the group.

Your prospect perceives you as enthusiastic when you are interesting and when you relieve, rather than contribute to, the tedium of the day. And when you do this, you feel refreshed as you refresh others. Your very manner and body language are positive—you come across as open, warm, sincere, and likeable.

You are perceived as enthusiastic when your prospects detect that you are genuinely interested in what they have to say—that you care about their interests, their opinions, their business, and their goals. Your enthusiasm shows when it is obvious that you have taken the time to learn about your prospect's business and to determine how your product or service might specifically fit. You don't have to feign this interest—it shows in your actions, manner, and posture.

PERSUASION KEY #5:
YOU FULLY EXPECT
THAT THE PROSPECT WILL BUY

With this attitude, you'll close more and you'll close sooner. It may mean that you'll have to psyche yourself up at times. But it's a fact: If your prospect sees you as confident that your product or service will deliver the promised benefits and confident of making the sale, you will be hard to resist. This confident feeling comes across in everything about you—the way you speak, the way you dress, and the way you carry yourself.

We, in the selling profession, are all actors at times. However, we are not actors in the sense that we pretend to a sincerity that we do not have. There are times, rather, that we will have to "play" at being more confident than we really are. We do this not for the purpose of deception, but simply to convince our own subconscious minds. Here is an important secret to remember: By repeatedly pretending to have courage, you develop courage. Act as though you are confident, and you will soon begin to *feel* confident!

There is no doubt about it; you can literally program almost any attitude into your subconscious. A rainy day can be dreary or it can be refreshing. It's not the day—it's your attitude. In Chapter 17, we'll go into a proven method by which we can maintain a high, positive, productive attitude every day.

Successful "wildcatters" are accustomed to drilling sometimes 10 holes before one results in a "strike," when oil comes gushing out. But there is the feeling that with each dry hole, striking oil is that much closer. And, here is the important thing about this: A wildcatter goes into each venture fully expecting to win. Truly, that is the attitude we need to develop in selling. Your attitude needs to be such that you fully expect to make the sale!

When you truly expect to make the sale, the prospect will pick up on your attitude and feel its compelling force. You then paint the kind of word pictures that help your prospects see themselves actually using and benefiting from your product or service. It no longer becomes a question of "if," but of "when, and how much."

3

The Art of Being
Pleasantly Pushy

Being pleasantly pushy is moving two steps forward, then one step back as you handle the rebuff or the rejection. Then two steps forward again, and again one step back. You're always moving toward your objective, but always in a warm, pleasant, understanding manner. You are always the lady or gentleman—never a pest or a bore.

Most salespeople would not physically grab a prospect by the arm, move close to a prospect's face, nor wag a finger, strut, or swagger. You can, however, convey these actions verbally if you're not careful.

Being careful about how we "push" means moving in a quiet, confident, poised, and professional manner. It is an attitude of calm warmth that comes across as delightful in its open courage. And, oh, how it closes sales!

It starts with making calls on the right people. To jump your income, it is critical that you are making your closing attempts on the right person. All it takes is being "pleasantly pushy" on the phone first to find out who the real decision maker is, when the best time is to make a personal call, what similar products or services are now in use, who else might influence a purchase, and what the buying procedure is.

EIGHTY PERCENT OF ALL SALES
ARE MADE AFTER
THE FIFTH CALL

Would you believe it? Yet, eighty percent of all salespeople quit after the third call! Taking advantage of the implications of this fact can decidedly increase your sales and your income. Think about it. Your competition is quitting after the third call. What a waste! And what a boon for you . . . knowing that your competition isn't following through.

I have learned from years of experience that when you hang in there, especially with a prime prospect, it really pays off. When someone says, "I'm not interested" or "We're happy with our present supplier" or "You're wasting your time," don't scratch that prospect. These are just words. Treat the challenge mathematically. You may be just one "return call" away from the sale.

There is an interesting psychological reason why most sales are closed after the fifth call. When we first meet, we are strangers. Yes, we smile and act friendly, but building confidence takes a while. Time is needed for the building of trust that comes only from a meshing of personalities. By the second call, we are acquaintances. Hopefully by the third call, we have begun to develop friendships. At the very least, each of us—prospect and salesperson—has developed a feeling of rapport for the other. And it is usual that this blossoming comes only to full flower by the fourth or fifth call.

In addition, there is a certain personality type that almost never buys on the first call. These people are often very warm individuals who want to get to know you as a person of integrity and loyalty. When they finally buy from you, they consider you a true friend and they trust what you do and say.

THINK "CLOSE"
ON EVERY CALL

If it takes that many calls, should you try to close on every call? Absolutely! If you decide not to go for the "final" close, at least take steps toward achieving it. Remember, if an average of 80 percent of calls are closed after the fifth call, 20 percent of sales were closed on perhaps the *eighth* call or the *fifteenth* call, as well as some that were closed on the very first call. And you'll certainly never experience the thrill of a "first-call close" unless you try for it!

Certain products, of course, almost always require several calls before a close is possible. If you were selling microprocessing equipment which had to be "specified," or "spec'ed," into the manufacturer's final product, you would probably make many calls before a "final close" could be made.

In such cases, there would likely be several "sales" that you would have to make before the final sale. You would probably have to sell a design or project engineer, someone in production, purchasing, and perhaps top management. One very large high-tech firm in California reports that the average sale takes about 18 months!

Make no mistake about it—selling is hard work. When we talk about five calls before a close, we're talking about five *personal* calls—not four telephone calls and one personal call. However, it may be economically or geographically impossible to make five face-to-face calls on a particular prospect. You will have to plan a mix of mail and telephone contacts with personal calls.

PLAN YOUR CALL PATTERN
AND STAY WITH IT

To close more and larger orders, decide on the number of calls that you can economically make on a prime prospect before giving up. Once you have decided on your pattern, stick with your decision, no matter what. Remember, selling is an art, but it is also a science and as such is subject to mathematical principles such as the law of averages—and of large numbers. You will get rebuffs from certain prospects and be tempted to deviate from your pattern, but stand firm and be patient.

If the sale could mean repeat business, you may even want to make six face-to-face calls before giving up. Some businesses with high repeat potential would be paper products, printing, goods for retail stores, chemicals, advertising, food products, banking, insurance, and stocks and bonds. If the geographic area is large, a reasonable limit of face-to-face calls might be twc, with perhaps three phone calls and three letters. But whatever you decide on, *stick with it!*

You might also set a six-call pattern where a large capital investment is required. Examples of this might be printing presses, industrial machinery, mainframe computers, and so on. In some cases, at least 10 calls might be justified, particularly where a number of influences are involved.

The number of calls must be economically justified. If the profit is only a few hundred dollars, and there is little or no potential for repeat business, then probably one call is all you should make. Much direct selling of books, vacuum cleaners, sewing machines, and alarm systems falls into this category. The salesperson must close on that first meeting. For the one-call closer, there is a specific technique that I call "response selling." This effective method is described in more detail in Chapter 11.

Every selling situation is different, so to get your own pattern, pull your call reports and get a reading on the number of calls it has taken to make the average sale. Call-backs must be interesting, not just repetitive. Nothing is more boring or a greater waste of time to a prospect than to hear the same spiel over and over again. Being "pleasantly pushy" and making five or six calls with nothing new to say isn't possible: you can be pushy that way, but not very pleasant.

Here is where brains and ingenuity come in: You must plan ahead for the probable number of call-backs you'll have to make. At the same time, you'll be planning how to close on each call or how to move the prospect closer to the final commitment.

You May Want Only to Probe on Your First Call

This is a good time to determine wants and needs. Remember, you're still a stranger, and you need to develop rapport. As a rule, make the first call short. You want to lock into the prospect's mind the notion that you're not the sort of person who wastes precious time. It makes it much easier to get that second appointment. Judgment dictates here: You may decide to go right into the close. Chapter 11 will discuss how to spot the signals that let you know when it's time to close it out.

Don't give him everything you've got on the first call—save something to talk about on the next call. And here's another tip: Never smoke on the first call, even if your prospect does. Keep small talk to a minimum. If this is a "probing" call, you'll probably need to set up an appointment for the second call, when you will present your plan.

Thoroughly study your proposition and how it relates to your prospect's needs. Pick up any brochures or other material you may want to use for this purpose, and read it through *seven times* before you make your next call. I know that sounds tedious. But what a difference it will make in your effectiveness! Key information will be locked into your subconscious and will bubble forth as needed during your presentation. Do this and you will overcome the number one gripe of buyers: "Salespeople won't take the time to understand our business."

Follow every first call with a short "enjoyed meeting you" note.

If you're in the field, do it in longhand on your company's letterhead. A note like this can give a buyer a nice, warm feeling—unless your handwriting is really atrocious!

On Your Second Call,
You Become an "Acquaintance"

Your second call may have been set up at your first meeting. But maybe you tried to close the sale and were turned down. Now you must call for another appointment even though you were turned down on the first call. Say something like this to get the appointment:

> YOU: Mr. Johnson, when we talked a few weeks ago, there was some-thing I meant to cover. Are you going to be in about 4:15 or 4:30 tomorrow afternoon? I'd like to drop by and get your opinion on something I wanted to show you.
> PROSPECT: Well, I'll be here, but really . . . I don't think that we'll be making any changes, as I told you when you were here.
> YOU: I understand. And I'm not talking about a lot of time. But I really would like your input on something I wanted to show you . . . so if it's OK, I'll make that about 4:15.
> PROSPECT: Well, alright, but like I said, I don't think we're interested at this time.
> YOU: Certainly, I understand that. I'll see you at 4:15 tomorrow.

And this is why you hold something back on that first call! You need something fresh to show on the follow-up. It doesn't have to be some-thing fantastic; it could be nothing more than showing the prospect a testimonial letter and "getting his opinion" on a similar solution to *his* problems. In spite of what your prospect has said up to now, you will go into this new call with the "100 percent attitude" that *you are going to close*. But, let's just say that you try for a close and you are turned down. Now, what do you do? You make a *third* call. Of course, it is assumed this is an excellent prospect—that the *potential* is worth the time and effort.

Three Calls Build
a Friendly Relationship

Three weeks pass from your second call. It's time for the third call. Of course, the actual space between this series of calls will vary according to what you sell. If you were trying to persuade a grocery chain to handle some of your products, you might see the buyer every week for perhaps six weeks. However, this might give you the reputation of a pest with a variety of prospects. Beyond a month, your face and name may become a vague memory. As a general rule, figure the series to be once every three weeks. This may be impossible if you're covering a large area; in that case, you might substitute a telephone call or a letter. Your prospect's mind must retain a sharp awareness of you.

For Closing Impact,
Use a Client List
of Six Names

Here is a powerful sales tool. You may want to use a client list for the third call-back. On your letterhead, prepare a list of six companies that are good customers. Include the contact name and the phone number of each company. If you are selling to individuals rather than to companies, then your list might also mention the person's occupation. Your list should include only customers who seem to like you very much personally. Clear it with each one and be sure that it's OK to use them as references. Let them know that they might be getting some phone calls.

Here's how you use your list: Call your prospect and let him know that you have something to drop by his office. Your conversation might go like this:

YOU: I understand that you're not really ready to buy now, but I've got something I'd like for you to look over . . . it could be very useful to you when and if you ever do decide to buy.

When you get to your prospect's office, your comment would be along these lines:

YOU: Jim, I know you said you weren't ready to buy yet. But I'd like you to take a look at this. Here, this second name on the list . . . they had a supplier that had been taking care of them for five years. We made several calls and they decided to go with us. They are so happy that they did . . . here's what they told us . . .

Now you would recite a number of benefits that the referenced customer has enjoyed. Then you'd turn his attention to maybe the fourth name on the list and explain why that person didn't buy at first— possibly he didn't want to spend money at that time. Explain how you made several calls on him before he decided to buy. Here again, you explain that he, too, is happy that he made the decision. And once again, you go through the benefits that the client has experienced.

You have done three things with this tool: 1) you have built credibility by showing a list of customers; 2) you have used the powerful "third-person technique" in overcoming a possible objection . . . *plus* you have let this "third person" explain your benefits—through you; 3) you have added one more call to your mathematical pattern, and thereby made another contribution to the success of the law of averages.

You need to give your prospect a reason for each call you make, each appointment you ask for. Your fourth, fifth, and sixth calls might include an invitation to lunch. This would also be a good time for a joint call with your salesmanager. It's a good time to bring in any new visuals, or maybe a batch of testimonial letters. If there are any new items just released, or if there is a new use for your product, tell the prospect about it on one of these calls.

THE PERSON WHO SAID "NO" MAY BE GONE NEXT MONTH

Out of 1,000 decision makers only 453 will be on the same job one year from today! It's a fact, verified by marketing researchers on job changing. This is another reason why it is critical to set multi-call patterns with your better prospects.

A salesman who represented a manufacturer of catscan X-ray equipment became discouraged after several calls on a hospital administrator in New Orleans. He turned the account over to a new salesman who was trying to establish himself. Within a short time the new man turned in an order from the hospital.

What happened? Was the new salesman a better salesman? Did he do something different? Not really. What really happened was that the hospital got a new administrator! Sometimes there may be a personality conflict between the salesperson and the prospect. Maybe the prospect is one of those vacillating or procrastinating types. Hang in there!

Roy Nelson sells envelopes for Federal Envelope Company. After about the fifth call on one prospect, the prospect said, "I don't know why you waste your time calling on me. I've told you I'm satisfied with our present supplier. I don't ever intend to change."

Maybe so, Nelson thought. But things do change. And Nelson felt that one day this prospect would want better service and that little extra touch of quality . . . and Nelson was right. Just a few calls later, persistence paid off with an order. Roy Nelson's attitude has kept him in a high-earning position for many years.

After you have made your predetermined number of calls (five, six, or ten—whichever you have decided), it is a good idea to put those "excellent prospects" which you haven't sold into a file. Then, every four months make telephone contact with each of them. You'll be astonished at the number of personnel changes that have taken place. In many cases you will be talking to new decision-makers. And the circumstances for closing the sale may be quite different.

DON'T THINK YOUR COMPETITION HAS AN ACCOUNT LOCKED UP

I have talked to many decision-makers to learn what they like or dislike about salespeople. One thing that surprised me was that a lot of these decision-makers have gnawing feelings of resentment toward salespeople who think that they have accounts "locked up" just because they've serviced those accounts for several years.

Sometimes a salesperson who has had an account for a long time will become a little careless in the servicing, or become indifferent or perhaps too familiar with the buyer. Sometimes a disagreement or a service problem will cause a breach in the relationship. That could happen in the very week that you are making your fourth call on the prospect! Remember what happened to the sign company salesman in Tampa, Florida? The regular supplier had made a bad blunder. In this case, the new sales rep had hung in there until the third call, when he made the sale that put his company in the big leagues!

HERE'S THE KEY THAT CRUMBLES RESISTANCE

Mark this advice well. It is the key to high sales production. We can resist the salesperson who talks too much, and we can easily ignore the cocky or overbearing type. But what about those salespeople who present themselves well, who are confident yet modest? Who can resist those who ask questions in a warm and friendly manner, and who use the feedback they get to show specific benefits—persons who come across as honest and knowledgeable about us and our company, as well as about their proposition?

Certainly, they can be resisted . . . temporarily. But resistance starts to crumble on those really interesting follow-up calls—those that paint pictures of benefits in the mind. And the resistance really breaks down as we sense that this warm and sincere person fully anticipates and expects that we will buy.

Of course, it isn't easy being this kind of salesperson; it takes a high order of dedication to be consistently pleasantly pushy. It means being really tough on yourself by formulating a realistic call pattern and sticking to it. It means getting to the decision-maker directly instead of wasting time with the easiest person you can reach. And it means asking for the order until you get it, or until you're reasonably sure that your call pattern has taken you as far as it can with this particular prospect.

Being pleasantly pushy demands that you ask the right questions so that you understand the reason for rejection or indifference. It means holding the price under pressure and pushing for the larger order. It also means remaining in control so that you're able to decide against making a presentation under the wrong setting or circumstances.

And, yes, it is even telling a vacillating prospect what to do—pleasantly. It's using your imagination and doing the unusual.

4

Closing the Various "Personality" Types

Type-psychology has been the subject of controversy among psychologists for a number of years. We are all mixtures of such complexity that it is simply not accurate to label anyone as being a certain type of personality. However, there are certain behaviors which come up often enough for us to develop useful techniques for dealing with these patterns in people.

For example, one prospect may be pleasant, but doesn't say much and just puffs on a pipe while you talk. He may ask a few questions, but doesn't respond to your questions. Another prospect you call on an hour later is at first very gracious, then begins to interrupt you, impatiently demanding that you get to "the bottom line." Another constantly answers the telephone and gives directives to the secretary as you try to make your presentation.

Being able to recognize these behavior styles in prospects will be of great help to you in selling. People react differently as you try to close the sale. Of course, we all react favorably to genuine smiles, to approval, and to people or things that make us feel good about ourselves. Beyond the basic traits we all have in common, there are many shades of differences in the way we react. Thank goodness for this—it would indeed be a dull world if we were all alike.

The psychologist William M. Marston has done us a tremendous service in documenting these interpersonal differences. In his book, *Emotions of Normal People*, Marston shows how people usually fall into four basic styles of behavior. Within these four styles of behavior, there are varying intensities. Also, although one style may predominate, most of us have behavior characteristics that are common to more than one style.

William Marston's rather ponderous work has been much simplified through the effort of Dr. John Geier. Dr. Geier was also responsible for having Marston's book reprinted in 1979 by Persona Press, Inc., Minneapolis, Minnesota.

I have taken Marston's four behavior styles and translated these into buying and selling situations. As you read about these different characteristics, keep in mind the following:

1. *You will identify your own sales style.* As you deal with various prospects, you will learn to mesh your style with theirs. We all wear masks in dealing with others. Even without understanding the psychology involved, we all "read" people to some extent and modify our behavior to get certain things that we want—so there is certainly nothing phony in learning how to do this more efficiently. What we are doing here is identifying a specific behavior and learning how best to mesh with that behavior.

2. *You will be able to identify a prospect's key behavioral style.* You'll recognize many of your present clients and prospects as you read this. At this point you will be more aware of the behavioral clues that you are learning, and you will begin to consciously apply these insights to the process of closing sales.

3. *You will understand your co-workers better.* This new insight cannot help but give you greater understanding of people as well as give you a real feel for the best method to use in getting cooperation from others in your office.

THE DESA FORMULA

To better understand Marston's terminology, I have updated the meanings he used to identify the behavior styles. The four styles represented by the letters "D," "E," "S," and "A," stand for the words, "Dominant," "Expressive," "Solid," and "Analytical," respectively.

The Dominant Type

Steve Groggan is a salesman who worked for a medium-sized health-maintenance organization (HMO) that provided complete medical care for employee groups. For two months he had been trying to see Richard Nelms, the president of a high-technology company. Nelms had cancelled each appointment at the last minute, a probable tip-off to the behavioral style that Nelms was using. This time, however, Groggan had succeeded in seeing the elusive Nelms.

"Mr. Nelms will see you now," the secretary announced.

Steve Groggan walked in, Nelms stood up, shook Steve's hand, gave Steve an even gaze, and said, "Watcha got?"

It was obvious to Steve that this man wanted to get down to business immediately. Steve did just that. He began explaining that Nolms's employees would no longer have to fill out insurance forms— all they would have to do is present a card to one of the HMO's medical centers. Nelms began reading, then signing some letters on his desk. Steve stopped.

"Go ahead, I'm listening," said Nelms. Steve was polite, but firm.

"Mr. Nelms," he said, "I believe that this is too important to your company and to your employees. I'd really like for us to take a hard look at these benefits together."

Nelms shot him a sharp glance; then, with a bit more warmth, a smile crossed his face and his eyes softened slightly.

"OK, Groggan," he said, "Let's take a look at those benefits." An immediate, warm rapport developed. Steve had figured right: He was dealing with a "D" type.

The Dominant type likes power, prestige, and the challenge of individual accomplishment. This type of individual is:

Impatient—wants immediate results

Restless—seeks variety

Impulsive—likes to change things

Competitive—wants to move up and run things

Seeking freedom from control by others—will argue one minute and laugh the next

Direct, sometimes abrupt

Task-oriented rather than people-oriented—will do whatever is required to get the job done

The "D" type may lack empathy because of a high-ego. His desk is often a mess because so many things are happening at once; this productivity gives "D" a feeling of accomplishment. There may be a bit of arrogance in his makeup, and he'll sometimes get into trouble by overstepping the bounds of authority and breaking rules.

Salespeople of this type like challenges and aren't afraid of cold calls. However, their sales presentations may be too brief; in fact, one problem is a tendency to close too soon. This behavioral type often attaches little importance to such things as getting reports in on time. It may be a tendency to nonconformity, or a disdain for someone else's "idiotic" rules.

"Dominant" prospects want you to get right to the point—to get to the bottom line quickly and spare the details. Keep small talk and social niceties to a minimum when dealing with these prospects. Remember, too, they like directness and don't like evasive, mealy-mouthed people. They are frequently impulsive, decisive people themselves and so expect that you will exhibit these qualities when you close a sale. They have little respect for the salesperson who won't go for the close and ask for an order. A definite turndown by "D" can be a "yes" decision a week later; just be sure to always go in prepared to discuss a new idea. "D" is easily bored and becomes restless.

There are other clues to the "Dominant" behavioral type. Many of them are "workaholics" because their work is their love. However, they do like change and may have many interests. Being quick in reactions and responses, they will often form an instant like—or dislike—for you. Whichever it is, it usually sticks. These persons are not the best listeners; they will often interrupt or finish your sentence for you. They can be gracious, but listen for the authoritative inflections as they talk to others on the phone or in the office.

Since "Dominant" types are highly competitive, they are interested in anything that would give themselves or their companies a competitive edge. Their greatest fear: loss of control.

The Expressive Type

Steve Groggan's next appointment was with Blair Creighton, Chief Executive Officer (CEO) for a wine distiller. He had seen Creighton once, about two weeks prior to this call. At that first meeting, the CEO was very friendly—they'd talked about football and sports statistics. They got along great. In fact, Steve got that excited inner feeling that he was going to sell his program on this call. The man was certainly responsive to the benefits which Steve had laid out. Steve liked the way his prospect smiled, talked, nodded. . . .

However, as Steve presented certain visual material, he noticed that Creighton didn't seem to read any of the facts and benefits that Steve pointed out. In fact, he seemed to be thinking of something else, even though he appeared to nod his head at the right point. This prospect seemed to enjoy discussion of the proposition more than analyzing printed data concerning costs and convenience.

Blair Creighton didn't buy that day, but he left the door open for a follow-up call. Steve felt sure that he'd close on this one.

Creighton had accepted his invitation to lunch. Normally, Steve would have felt a bit presumptuous in suggesting lunch after having seen a prospect just once. However, the tasteful decor of Creighton's office, his outgoing manner, his easy sociability and love for conversation convinced Steve: Creighton was an "E" type.

Steve made a reservation at one of the finer restaurants. He had also prepared a simple, four-sheet presentation. The first sheet had Creighton's name on it; the second sheet was a list of nine large and prestigious firms that were customers of Steve's company; the third sheet spelled out the plan for Creighton's firm—the cost and the suggested starting date; the fourth sheet detailed particulars of the plan. The lines of type were double-spaced, without too much material on any one page. The whole presentation, with its blue and gold folder, had a touch of real class to it.

As Steve waited in the lobby, he heard Creighton laughing and talking as he came down the hall. Was he bringing someone else with him? Creighton greeted Steve warmly.

"Steve," he said, "Meet Jim Sherwood, our personnel manager. I thought it might be a good idea if he joined us."

This was a good sign, Steve thought. People in charge of human resources are frequently the ones in charge of employee group plans. Steve was glad he had decided to bring an extra copy of the presentation with him.

"Expressive," or "E" types are open, emotional, animated people.

> They are friendly, enthusiastic, entertaining, and "people oriented."
> They love to talk.
> Confident and with a high degree of ego, the "E" types like to wield authority, and strive for social recognition, prestige, and elegance.
> They're often stylish dressers.

This type prefers that everything be handled orally in lieu of written reports or proposals—they dislike filling out forms themselves. In fact, they tend to be sloppy with reports and forms and may make mistakes. Being restless and needing change and variety, there is often a difficulty "getting organized" and managing time. At times these people appear to be listening, but their thoughts are actually elsewhere. The "E" types are very trusting, lenient, optimistic and usually have a desire to help others. Frequently they live up to, or beyond their incomes—unless there is a blend with the more careful characteristics of "S" or "A" types.

You'll often see a touch of the "good life" in this person's office decor, and his choice of restaurants, dress, and car. Surroundings may get cluttered, but this "E" can easily get it all shoved into drawers if someone is coming to visit.

The "E" salesperson meets new prospects easily, is friendly, talkative, expressive, and instinctively knows how to make a good presentation. However, he has a tendency to "wing it" at times rather than being fully prepared. Every sales call is a social event. This person may talk beyond the point at which the buyer is ready to close. Reports from this type of salesperson are often late—and a bit sloppy and hard to read. There's also a tendency toward procrastination. These are people-oriented salespersons and their enthusiasm frequently sparks the atmosphere when they walk in. They get acquainted with others quickly, and like to visit. They need to watch their time and plan sales calls carefully.

"E" prospects like new ideas, new items, and new approaches. In identifying "E," look for the latest thing in status symbols. The way "E's" talk is a clue, too; they are apt to ramble onto various extraneous topics. "E's" dislike great detail and will usually skim over your most important (but for them too-detailed) figures or printed material. Don't be surprised if such material is practically ignored. For this reason "E's" are rarely encountered as buyers of high-tech material or equipment. Nor will you often find them as project engineers or tax consultants. "E" buyers are flexible and they'll compromise to get what they're after. They can overlook problems and adjust quickly.

"E" prospects are very friendly. As you walk in and the "E" type greets you, you may think, "Wow! I've got this sale wrapped up . . . this buyer really likes me!" And you'd be right; being optimistic, this prospect probably figures the two of you will do business sooner or later. But you're not the only person that this prospect likes. And, of course, this buyer can't buy from everyone.

The key to closing here is to let the prospect talk, then to maneuver the conversation into business channels, and from there into the details of your proposition. Drop the names of some of your more prestigious customers. And when you take the "E" type to lunch, you'll find that the food isn't as important as the atmosphere of the restaurant. Keep this type of prospect alive with immediate, friendly follow-up by phone, letter, and personal calls.

The Solid Type

Steve had one more call to make. He was to see Harold Johnson at 3:00 P.M. This would be his fourth call on Johnson, the senior partner in a large engineering firm. Steve liked this man; there was a warmth and sincerity about him that seemed special. But Steve still wasn't sure how Johnson felt about health maintenance organizations (HMO). In fact, Johnson seemed rather noncommital on the first two calls, although he did carefully review the HMO benefits on the third call. And he did finally agree to Steve's suggestion for putting together a specific proposal. On this call Steve hoped to get a commitment. Steve noticed some of the pictures on the wall in the lobby. They showed some of the various industrial plants which Johnson's firm had had a part in building.

Johnson came out into the lobby and greeted Steve. It was a quick greeting, but there was a real depth to this prospect—Steve felt this in the look in Johnson's eyes. Together they walked quietly back to Johnson's office. Steve took note of the orderly, almost spartan surroundings. Johnson sat and methodically filled and lit his pipe. Then he carefully began poring over Steve's written proposal. Steve was careful not to interrupt the man's reading. At length, the prospect leaned back in his chair.

"You know," he said to Steve, "we have a good group insurance plan already."

"Yes, I do know that," Steve answered. "And it is a good one."

Johnson pursed his lips in thought.

"Steve, I really wonder whether many of our people, particularly our engineers, would want to be treated by a doctor they don't even know. They're well covered by our group plan right now and can continue to use their own private doctors."

Steve remembered the pictures of the industrial plants he saw in the lobby.

"Mr. Johnson, in your construction projects do you also have a number of employees with limited education, or some who have some difficulty with the written language? The reason I mention this is that many people have difficulty filling out insurance forms. With this program, all they would have to do is present an ID card at one of our medical centers. Also, there are a number of doctors they can choose from. There is absolutely no paper work for them to do. And I'm not recommending that you drop your present group coverage. This is simply a convenient low cost option for those employees who want it rather than the group insurance plan. As you say, some may wish to continue the present coverage."

Steve felt this man had a lot of the "S" qualities—that he couldn't be pushed; that benefits had to be spelled out in a logical fashion.

Johnson studied Steve for a moment.

"Is your company the best HMO in the area?" he asked.

"Mr. Johnson," Steve replied, "I work for an excellent company . . . I wouldn't work for them otherwise. But there are other excellent HMOs in this area. We're not alone. However, when it comes to service, I will personally be your right hand. I'd certainly like to work with you. I'll be as close as that phone in servicing this account."

Johnson looked at Steve for quite awhile before saying anything. Then, with a twinkle in his eye, he said "How do you want to set up a presentation for the employees?"

Steve felt that the answer he'd given to Johnson's question about being the best HMO in the area went a long way toward bringing Johnson to this point.

The "S," or "Steady" type, is the most mature of the four types. These people:

> Display a quiet and controlled sort of warmth and friendliness—they are the best listeners of the four behavior styles.
> While outwardly undemonstrative, they feel deeply.
> Modest and unassuming, they are patient with others.
> They give (and expect) loyalty, and are consistently high performers.
> They like a structured approach in reaching decisions.
> Although easy-going and kind, they can't be pushed and can become stubborn and rigid when pressured or manipulated.

"S" types care about family, friends, neighbors, and people they know in school. They are the most generous when someone needs help. However, don't borrow something from them without asking. They dislike sudden changes in job, conditions, or friends. Security for themselves and their families is of utmost importance.

Never explain the end result to this type without clearly outlining the steps that will be taken to reach that result. Genuine friendships mean a great deal to "S," whether socially or in business. But cross the "S" type person once, and it will never be forgotten.

The "S" salesperson is warm, loyal, honest, low-key, and well-prepared. Such salespeople have empathy and understanding for the prospect. They don't set excessively high expectations for the performance of others; therefore, they have great tolerance and understanding of their prospects and clients. They are the ones who get along best with all of the other types. An "S" will follow up and follow through. They are mature in their work habits, and they'll put in a full day regardless of supervision. The "S" doesn't like showoffs and is careful not to be one. Because he is so good at service and follow-up, this type of salesperson is tough for the competition to dislodge.

The "S" prospect will usually not buy on the first call. This prospect needs time to get to know salespeople who call on him in order to gauge their integrity. He prefers to continue buying from the same salesperson, barring poor performance or a broken promise. Two words mean almost everything to this type: integrity and loyalty. He will be looking for signs of these qualities as he listens to your presentation. This can be frustrating for the salesperson, as "S" sits impassive and expressionless. Perhaps even worse, the "S" prospect's response to questions are limited and hard to draw out. Once sold, however, he is loyal and supportive. Never exaggerate a claim, even by a little bit, with this person. And back up claimed benefits with good "reason-why" material. Appeal to this type with good security reasons.

The Analytical Type

Steve had an 8:30 A.M. meeting at Goodman Tekmold, a firm that makes housings for computers, CRT screens, and printers. It was Steve's second call on Larry Goodman, the owner. Goodman had been friendly enough on the first call, and even showed Steve through the plant. Goodman was obviously proud of what he had built in just 10 years. He'd started as a chemical engineer, used his knowledge of fiberglass and plastics, and had put together a fast-growing company. But Goodman didn't seem too interested in HMOs. Steve had pressed for this return visit.

Traffic was heavy this morning. Steve looked at his watch; it was 8:18. He wasn't far from the Goodman plant, but at the rate traffic was moving, he would probably be a few minutes late. Better call, he thought. He turned off the freeway and found a phone at a gas station. When he walked into Goodman's office five minutes later, he was greeted with a warm smile. Steve had a feeling that Goodman had appreciated the call, even though he was only a few minutes late. Goodman looked like an "A" type—a perfectionist, Steve thought. Goodman's appointment diary lay open with neat entries in it. There was one letter at the corner of the desk and in front of Goodman was a blank legal pad.

On this call Steve planned to present several testimonials from satisfied clients. Goodman listened for a bit, then asked Steve how long his company had been in business and how many medical centers the company operated. He asked where the centers were and the total enrollment at each—all questions which probed into the financial stability of Steven's firm as well as his company's ability to give efficient service.

One of Steve's remarks on labor problems caught Goodman's attention. Steve remembered how a customer of his had avoided a labor problem by offering this plan to his employees. Steve told Goodman about it, and as Steve anticipated, Goodman wanted to know more.

Goodman asked Steve to return with an exact breakdown of costs on four separate plans: plans which showed the cost to the company where the company paid 100 percent, 75 percent, 50 percent, and 25 percent of the premium. Goodman also wanted a complete history of Steve's company, together with a list of customers, showing how long each customer had been with Steve's HMO. Goodman said that he planned to present the plan for discussion at the next board meeting, in about three weeks.

Steve felt good about this call. He liked the preciseness of Goodman's questions. True, there had been no commitment yet. But Steve knew his business, and he'd answered Goodman's questions well. The next step, he knew, was to get a *detailed* presentation into Goodman's hands—and to do this within a couple of days, not in two weeks. Then, after going over this presentation with Goodman, he would at least try for permission to be present at that board meeting— ready to answer any questions that came up.

> The "A," or "Analytical" type, strives for perfection, whether it's in sports, medicine, or business.
>
> "A's" are planners and problem solvers, and follow directions precisely, exemplifying quality control and accuracy.
>
> "A's" are critical thinkers, especially good at analyzing people, things, and figures.
>
> Emotions influence "A's" as they do other types, but "A's" are capable of deeper, more penetrating analysis of factual data. They will almost always have a back-up, or alternative plan of action.

Analytical types are also intuitive and inclined to worry, since they frequently see potential problems before others do. Never bluff this type. With friendly, soft-spoken, but exacting questions, "A's" can back a bluffer right into the corner. Diplomatic themselves, they don't like overly aggressive people; neither do they like careless or disorderly people. Doctors, CIA agents, and high-tech people frequently possess characteristics of the "A."

"A" salespeople are thorough and reliable. These people are particularly excellent in the sale of high-tech goods or services. Because they are analytical, they tend to present propositions in a clear, concise, and logical fashion. Prospects can tell almost at once that these people know what they're doing and have done their homework. Such salespeople are problem solvers for their prospects. "A's" dislike pushing hard for a close; instead, they prefer to let the pros and cons of the proposal speak for themselves. When selling to impatient "D's" or to "E's," "A" salespeople may need to be careful to hold back details, as "D" or "E" will likely stop listening if the presentation is too detailed.

"A" prospects have the knack of asking key questions, and they have an uncanny way of getting to the truth. Quiet and amiable themselves, they dislike pushy salespeople. As they ask their questions, things fall into place for them like the pieces of a jigsaw puzzle. Perhaps a piece will fail to fit. They won't argue or call you a liar because they generally dislike confrontations. Instead, they'll just tell you they're not interested. And since they detest mistakes, they will look for solid assurances, facts, proof, and testimonials.

Don't be even one minute late to an appointment with this type of person—tardiness is a sign of sloppiness. Since they plan everything carefully, they expect you to do the same. And just because an error seems insignificant to you, don't count on it getting by this person's watchful eye.

A neat desk is another clue to this type (unless they happen to be buried under a heavy workload.) "A's" car is probably kept in meticulous condition. In fact, everywhere you look in this person's environment, you will usually find things neat and in order.

The Blend of Various Types*

Most people are blends of the four types. For example, a blend of an "E" with an "A" would be very neat and organized, yet outgoing. A blend of "A" and "S" would be clear thinking and possibly a stubborn realist who can't stand mediocrity in himself or in others. A person with a blend of "D" and "A" would be creative and demanding—a planner who is expansive one day and coldly analytical and picky the next.

Not only are there many blends, but there are degrees of these blends, so the variations are numerous. One cannot expect to get a clear picture of the exact behavior type by just sitting and talking with a prospect for a few minutes. Speech, manner, writing, questions, dress, desk—all give clues. Because the four behavior types react a bit differently in the selling process, those clues that are picked up will prove most helpful in getting the final commitment to buy.

*A person's personality style, and various combinations and intensity of behavior may be determined through a word association instrument called the DESAnalysis. The DESAnalysis can be ordered in quantities from Patton Communications, Inc., 3000 Wilcrest, Suite 145, Houston, TX 77042.

Which Type Makes
The Best Salesperson?

There is no clear answer to this because much depends on what the person is selling. The person doing high-tech selling, calling on project engineers, data-processing department heads, or doctors, would probably have a blend of "S" or "A."

On the other hand, encyclopedia salespeople would need to have some "D" in their makeup. "D" people don't like slammed doors or rejections, but they can handle it better than other types. A "D" would probably make an obscene gesture at the slammed door and go to the next house.

5

How to Develop
a Super Phone Personality

Your phone personality is one of the most important areas in selling—and this isn't limited to inside phone salespeople. The outside salesperson has to sell the appointment, and frequently has to follow up with some selling on the phone. The executive, too, is continually influencing people, handling objections and complaints, and selling ideas on the phone.

We use the phone to gather information, to find out who the decision maker is, and to make good appointments with the right persons. We use it to service accounts, to close more sales with existing accounts, and to find and close new prospects. Is it any wonder that our success as salespeople is so profoundly influenced by the way we come across on the phone?

This chapter will show you how to improve your telephone personality; it will show you how to listen with a keener perception to what your prospect is saying, thereby sharpening your winning edge in selling and closing on the phone!

Let's start by studying these ten detractions from a good phone personality:

1. Speaking in a flat, monotonously-dull voice.
2. Mushy, or indistinct words, poor enunciation.
3. Meanings are not clear and to the point.

4. Slow in getting to the purpose of the call—rambling on and on.
5. Unfinished sentences, constantly interrupting self with new thoughts.
6. Not listening with concern, or simply pretending to listen as mind wanders.
7. Too many "ah's," "ya know's," "OK's" or constant nervous giggling or laughing.
8. Ponderous, repetitious or slow pace.
9. Boring. Too much talk about self or too much detail.
10. Lack of empathy. Not sensing when prospect is in a meeting, in a hurry, or busy.

As you study this list, you may find one or two areas in which you consider yourself "just average." If this is the case, get to work on the following plan. Your objective is to be exceptional—in the top 5 percent of all salespeople!

THE FIVE-WEEK PLAN

This plan will make a decided difference in your selling and closing results.

You will need a cassette tape recorder—it doesn't have to be an expensive one. Starting tomorrow, put a blank 30-minute tape in it and set it near your telephone. Turn it on when you are ready to make a number of phone calls. Since it is not connected to the telephone, and you are taping only your side of the conversation, you needn't mention the recorder to the party at the other end of the line.

When you play the recording back, you will probably find that you sound great for the first ten minutes or so. Then, as you forget about the recorder, your old phone habits will start to creep in again. Listen to the tapes after work, but don't be too hard on yourself: Try to be objective. Perhaps you rambled a bit as you spoke, and some of your sentences trailed off.

Do this 30-minute recording just once a week for five weeks. In the evening, listen to the tape you have made that day. Your subconscious mind will spot those areas in which improvement is needed, and gradually—without conscious effort—wrong habits will be obliterated. You'll start getting more of an "upswing" in the last few words in each sentence. Eventually there will be more variation in sentence structure; your words will be more interesting. The "I like you" attitude will come through with warmth. Perhaps for the first time, you will hear yourself *smile*! You will listen, perceive, and react better. Much of the anxiety will be gone from your voice; you will likely have lost most of your fear of closing by telephone! You will feel far more confident as you are able to handle objections and turndowns with ease. And, best of all, you will close more, and you will close more quickly.

This "mind programming" is done by affirming to yourself, before each call you make, certain statements outlined below. You will do this every day for the *first* and *third* weeks of the program. If this sounds tedious, think how much time you would spend conditioning yourself to play, say, the *Moonlight Sonata* on the piano.

On the first day, use the same affirmation to yourself before each call, whether you make 10 calls or 40. Then you will change the affirmation for each succeeding day. What do you affirm to yourself? Read the suggestions in the WICKS program, which follows.

THE WICKS PROGRAM

Using the WICKS affirmations, you condition your mind to make subtle changes in the way you come across on the telephone. You will notice changes in your manner of delivery and your phrasing. You will come across as warmer and more persuasive. Remember, the affirmations are made only on the *first* and *third* weeks.

Here are the affirmations:

DAY ONE   "I am *warm*. I like you and want to help you." Remember to say this before each call you make. On every call you make this day, you are programming into the subconscious mind an attitude of warmth and caring. Your sales presentation will be centered around benefits and around satisfying emotional wants.

DAY TWO   "I am *interesting* because I am *interested* in you." With this affirmation, you are programming in the habit of concern about what your prospect really wants. Remember, give people what they want and they will give you what you want.

DAY THREE   "I am crystal *clear* in what I say. I am totally straightforward with you." By this affirmation, you are programming in distinct, clear speech. You begin to make plain what benefits your proposition conveys and what you expect in exchange.

DAY FOUR   "I am *kind*. I understand how you feel." Your subconscious becomes impressed with the attitude of empathy, and you become strongly motivated to help your prospect overcome the usual fears (objections) which cause a reluctance to buy.

DAY FIVE   "I am *spontaneous*. I feel very open with you. I think you are great." You are now building in an attitude of open honesty and enthusiasm toward your prospect or client. Don't be surprised if your voice takes on a new lilt, a sort of bounce that hadn't been there before. Spontaneity gives a freedom from the kind of conscious fretting that drags one down. It is that quality that makes youth so appealing.

Start at once to put this program into effect. Remember, you record all your outgoing calls once a week for thirty minutes. Then, during the first and third weeks, add the WICKS program. At the end of five weeks, compare your first tape with your last tape.

YOUR SMILE WILL
DOUBLE YOUR SALES

We have made a number of tests to determine the effect that a smile has on the voice of the speaker. There is no question about it—you will do twice as well with a smile as you will without it! If you don't believe it, try it for yourself. Make 25 phone calls without smiling and another 25 presentations with a smile. Smile *the entire time* you are on the telephone. It won't work by just smiling during the introductory sentences, or by just smiling halfway through.

Smiling all the way through isn't easy; it takes practice. Some people consider this kind of smile "phony." In a sense, you might call it that. It is phony in that you might have to start smiling before you actually experience the emotional tone that smiling induces. Once you really get into it, however, it won't seem artificial at all. A top sales pro selling advertising in Texas is Mary Zarsky. Her earnings are in the six-figure bracket. Mary says she not only smiles at her prospects over the telephone, she smiles at herself! Here's how she does it:

> I've been doing this for about 10 years now. If it's "phony," then having fun is phony! I have a mirror set up so that I can see myself as I talk on the phone. I smile at myself as well as at my prospect as I talk. I tell you, it works. People who work around me tease me about it sometimes. Once somebody stole my mirror. But I'm serious about it; I know that smiling makes a difference in the way I sound over the telephone.

Mary Zarsky's experience is reinforced by the experience of countless others, including my own. I know from my own experience that there is much in every business relationship to be happy about; there is much that is worth a genuine smile. And there is no more "pretense" involved here than there is in being pleasant with everyone. There is nothing artificial in this, any more than there is something artificial in trying to modulate and improve the effectiveness of one's voice, or, for that matter, in the whole process of influencing people.

It may help you to better understand this if you consider just what's happening in these situations. First, realize that what you are saying on the telephone constitutes an emotional experience for you and your listener. Consciously and subconsciously, your listener is instantly forming feelings of like and interest, or dislike. Logic has very little to do with it. Almost the entire interaction is on a feeling level. Your smile gives a slight lift or upturn to each word you use. Each word you use can be "wrapped" with feelings—feelings that will convey the message "I like you," and your entire presentation will receive a more favorable response.

But don't take my word for it; try it yourself. Put a mirror directly in front of you like Mary Zarsky does. Seeing yourself as you talk is a tremendous aid in maintaining the "smiling voice" from start to finish. The mirror will also help you by stimulating you to produce gestures which, although they can't be seen by the other party, give life and verve to your voice. You will probably find yourself becoming more spontaneous and far less stilted.

PARALINGUISTICS AND THE ART OF READING PEOPLE

The word "paralinguistic" is formed by combining the word "linguistic," which refers to the study of language, with the Greek derivative "para," which means "at the side of." In essence, it is the study of meanings that seem to exist alongside the words that are spoken. Paralinguistics might be considered the "body language of the vocal chords." Like "body language," paralinguistics seem to catch real meanings that are sometimes hidden as we consider the overt meanings of the words we hear.

That our emotions color and give substance to the words we use is probably beyond question. For the most part, we can control what we say; controlling certain subconscious acts of the body is something else, however. You will recognize that this fact provides the rationale behind such devices as the polygraph machine and the voice stress analyzer. What is important is the fact that we can, through the practice of careful listening, determine what prospects or clients really *mean* through what they *say*.

The telephone offers a special advantage to the careful listener. When you listen on the phone, you aren't distracted by visual impressions. It doesn't matter how people are dressed, how old they are, or what they look like. Also, you will find that your listening is of a different order: It will tend to be far more concentrated and much sharper. You will probably find, when listening on the telephone, that you can more accurately pick up on whether a prospect is interested or uninterested than if you were speaking to him or her face to face.

Sensitivity to paralinguistics takes total concentration, but you will find it fascinating! Begin to practice it with your very next phone call. Your desire to succeed will heighten your awareness of the many shades of meaning possible for each word that your client or prospect uses. You will find that it is very difficult for you or for anyone else to disguise feelings over the phone.

Five Things You Must Do
To Read Paralinguistic Signals

1. *Check your environment.* Make sure that there is nothing around you that could break your concentration. If you're calling from home, be sure that there's no radio or TV to distract you. Arrange so that your spouse will not disturb you. If calls are being made from your office, you may need to do some special things to secure the kind of quiet you need; whatever it takes, *do it.* You need to achieve an atmosphere of almost *total isolation.*

2. *Control your thoughts.* This is far easier said than done. Yet, it is crucial to your practice. It is so easy to wander off . . . to become lost in your own thoughts while someone is talking to you. Perhaps this will not happen to you if you really convince yourself how vitally important it is that you give total and complete attention to the voice on the other end of the line. Just remember that the price for mind drifting may well be that you will miss the key part of your prospect's message; that part, perhaps, which is giving you certain directions on what to do or what to say.

3. *Control your enthusiasm.* Yes, you need to be enthusiastic. But you *don't* need uncontrolled enthusiasm. You don't need the kind of exuberance that can dampen your sensitivity to the messages that are coming through from the other person.

4. Listen for a "turning down" of word endings or sentence endings. If you really listen, you will hear when there is discouragement, lack of interest, or fear. Listen, too, for the up-turned words that indicate interest, liking, and optimism. Listen for temerity or guilt. Pessimism, frustration, guilt, and anxiety often come through as a sigh. Pay attention to the way your prospect says another person's name. If you listen, you can identify the character of your prospect's relationship with that other person. With practice, you will be able to hear jealousy, resentment, and fear.

5. Listen actively; this encourages the flow of messages. You do this by

responding with short questions such as, "Really?" or "How come?" and "You did? How? No kidding!"

Of course, you will remember to keep a smile in your voice throughout the conversation. And keep lifting your prospect with those verbal strokes that say "I like you." It's really as easy as remembering to keep dropping comments like, "Jim, you stay really tuned to trends. What are your feelings about . . ."

Keep these tips in mind as we move into the next chapter, which will show you how to set up an effective telephone system.

6

How to Set Up
a Phone System

The telephone enormously increases the number of prospects that you can contact. Not only that, but you can quickly identify which are your best prospects. And you do this while avoiding traffic, waiting in offices, and wasting time talking to the wrong people.

With the telephone, you quickly determine who makes the decision and where that decision is made—the decision on whether or not to buy your product or service. With a few well-chosen questions, you can find out if your "suspect" is really a worthwhile prospect. In just a few seconds more, you can learn who your competition is. And on the telephone you can plow right through the barricade of screens, right through to "Mr. Right."

In spite of the obvious benefits of the telephone as a sales tool, many salespeople sidestep it entirely in gathering information and in closing sales. Some dread using the telephone to make appointments for fear that they can be too easily rejected. Perhaps it is the fear of the unknown, or perhaps it is just that they simply feel better making contacts in person, face to face. Many salespeople claim that they are more persuasive in person than on the phone.

What is the truth of the matter? Do prospects prefer the face-to-face approach? Some may, but experiments conducted by researchers at the University of Nottingham found that strong, persuasive points presented on the telephone produced higher results than did those same points presented in person. The evidence suggests that people are distracted more in a visual presentation, and that on the telephone, strong points get through and register.

USING THE TELEPHONE
TO REACH THE DECISION MAKER

Would you believe that 68% of all sales calls are made on the wrong persons? What a waste of time! Before you make your first face-to-face call, you need to find out who the *real* decision maker is. It may not be the one that the receptionist gives you. And a person's title may be meaningless as far as determining whether you are talking to the person who can buy what you are selling. You need information about what they're using now and how they like what they're using. Here's a unique method that gets the right names and the information you need.

Make your first call to your targeted prospective company to a person who would not be involved in the purchase of your product or service. For example, you might call and ask for the sales manager. Your call might go something like this:

Mr. Thompson, this is Dick Simpson. I'm with the American Forklift Company. I need your help. I'm planning to make a presentation out there in the next day or two. Who makes the final decision in buying forklift trucks?

Now why would the sales manager be more disposed to help you than, say, a receptionist? Well, for one thing, a sales manager usually knows the exact political structure of a company—who the influencers and decision makers are. Sales managers are usually warm and helpful— and they understand and appreciate this kind of qualifying approach. You might have noticed the use of one magic little sentence that almost compels attention. It has only four words in it, but it is one of the most powerful sentences you can use in selling: "I need your help." Just four words, but they will get you past screens, win you important selling information, and get you instant cooperation.

Your sales manager contact would probably know such things as how many trucks were already in use in the warehouse, possibly the brand used, as well as the average age of the trucks. But let's continue with our example to further clarify the operation of this truly useful technique. Remember, you have just asked who the decision maker is. The sales manager might reply:

"Well, Dick, you're going to have to see Ed Wilcox in purchasing."

"Would Ed Wilcox make the *final* decision?" you ask.

"Actually, our warehouse superintendent, Nick James, would also have to OK any purchase like that. He's been with us about 15 years and always OK's everything like that. But I don't think they're in the market for forklifts. They've got several Yorks that are only about five or six years old. And they have some at the other warehouse," Thompson tells you.

"The other warehouse?" you respond.

"We have a smaller one out on East River Road," he says. "They're in the process of adding on to that one."

You still have to make another call—one to the decision maker—but you are now armed with such a wealth of pertinent information that you can begin to plan an effective presentation.

In addition to the sales manager, you will probably find that there are several other "nonbuyers" who can furnish you with the information you need. If the sales manager isn't in when you call, you might try the head bookkeeper or the executive secretary. Either of these people would likely know who the final decision maker is. Also, people who are *inside sales* can be very helpful; they frequently know the "political" structure of the business; they know what's going on—and that's what *you* need to know.

These "insiders" can often furnish you with information on competition, dissatisfactions, the state of the business, the best time for contact, and the company's goals and markets. In fact, in just two or three minutes on the telephone you will be able to gather enough information to help make a very effective face-to-face presentation.

Just be sure never to forget those four magic words: *I need your help.*

USE THE PHONE TO SERVICE ACCOUNTS

Make a telephone follow-up immediately after delivery. It not only builds confidence in your company, but it may stop a molehill of a problem before it grows into a mountain. You'll be checking to make sure that installation was up to specifications, whether there are any questions concerning operation, and if it was delivered as agreed and in good condition. This call can also get you additional business and referrals. Just think how you would feel if you had just opened a bank account and you got a welcoming call from one of the bank's vice presidents! How nice it would be to get a "check up" call from the salesperson who had just sold you a car! What terrific public relations it would be for the furniture store, department store, or insurance company to just make that one little follow-up call!

Here's another tip. Always send a thank-you note right after you have made the sale. This need not be more than two or three lines. And don't overlook the impact of two short letters: one from you, and one from your president or from someone in top management.

Your very best prospects are your present customers. Make regular phone calls to increase business. Be careful that you don't succumb to the negative impact of that old saw: "Don't mess up a good thing." Don't fear asking for more business just because you don't want to seem greedy. Remember, your customer already has confidence in you. You already have important knowledge about that customer's needs. *Do* ask for more business—if you don't, your competitor will. Continually probe for ways that additional products or service can help. Get names of people in other departments or divisions of the company. Ask. People like to help, but they have to be asked. And ask for referrals from every customer you have. Consider the mathematics involved in an endless chain started by getting just three referrals from every customer. By showing constant interest, you will virtually freeze out the competitive attempts at your customers. And regular phone calls allow you to maintain this friendly relationship.

Brandon Wilcox, a top salesman for a large packaging company, has nine key customers. They represent the big fruit and vegetable packers in the Rio Grande Valley. He keeps in touch with each one every day because each customer represents a lot of annual business. He has made a personal friend of each of his buyers, and he knows all of their day-to-day problems, whether they be of a business or personal nature. When he entertains the men who buy from him, he includes the man's wife and children!

TREAT EACH INQUIRY
AS IF A CLOSE FRIEND IS CALLING

Many people "window-shop" by telephone before actually buying. For this reason, you can expect to get some calls that will never result in a sale for you or your company. However, there is virtually no way that you can determine whether an inquiry is being made by a serious prospect who is ready and willing to buy, or whether the person is simply "window-shopping."

Your concern, then, is that you treat every inquiry in such a manner that, wherever possible, you will convert the "shopper" into a buyer. And at the very least, you will offend no one. The secret here is warmth. Remember to use the same techniques of smiling and gesturing that you do on your out-going phone calls.

My wife, Nelle, is one of the leading real estate agents in the Houston area. She trains many of the new agents in special techniques in handling real estate inquiries. When people call various real estate companies, they frequently don't identify themselves. Therefore, to gain the competitive edge it is essential to get their name and know where to reach them. She would handle an inquiry something like this:

"This is Nelle Patton. May I help you?" She says it slowly with a smile in her voice.

"What's the price of that house on Ella Lane?" someone asks.

Now it is at this point that "opportunity" flies right over the heads of many salespeople. There are two very common faults practiced in this situation. Fault number one is giving a quick, direct answer to the price question. Fault number two is attempting to *withhold the price* in the face of a direct request! Here's how you can avoid both of these faults.

"The house on Ella Lane? I don't have the complete file in front of me. Let me have your name and telephone number. I'll get the file so I can answer all of your questions, and I'll call you right back."

Warmth is important here, but so is affirmative strength. The above is a powerful technique to not only secure the name and number, but to hold the prospect. Some callers slur their own names when talking over the telephone. If this happens, don't hesitate to say, "I'm sorry, I didn't catch that . . ." And if it's still difficult to understand, be quick to come back with a warm, interested request for the caller to repeat the name. Blame it on a bad connection, ask him to spell it if you have to, but get the name right!

Most inquiries can be followed by a direct close, or by questions that can lead to a direct close. For example, a salesperson has just received a telephone inquiry on the price of the store's best band saw. Here's how he converted the inquiry into a sales opportunity:

"Mr. Thompson, the price is $897.00, but let me ask you— would you be using this for hardwood or softwood?"

You see, questions give you feedback, get the prospect involved, and keep you in control. If this salesperson had simply responded with the price, the caller would have said, "Thank you" and hung up to continue shopping around. Questions (and answers), however, lead naturally into the close.

Let's examine how questions can lead into closings. Remember, we asked whether the prospect would be using the saw on hardwood or softwood. Let's assume the caller said he would be using the saw on hardwood.

"Hardwood? One of our customers had been using a saw without the X2 grip features this saw has. He was totaling up many wasted man-hours in changing blades. And this saw is rugged—built to last. There are special features that make it easier to operate, too, that can be important when you have new people on a crew. If you'll just give me a PO number, I'll be sure to get this out by tomorrow morning."

Of course, your prospect may not be ready to close this quickly and you may have to give him some additional reasons for buying. You are probably accustomed to doing this in face-to-face selling, but perhaps hadn't thought of trying it on telephone inquiries as well. Try it! After giving a few more buying reasons, you might finish like this:

"Mr. Thompson, many lumber companies who buy this saw order it with the special extender. This way, they don't have to take time to change blades as frequently. The extender is only $32.50. Shall we include an extender?"

Your sales conversation may even continue past two attempted closes while you continue to give more reasons for buying. If this happens, you will want to change your closing question again.

"We can get that out either this afternoon or tomorrow morning. What is your shipping address, Mr. Thompson?"

A prospect will often say something like, "I want to think about it," instead of giving you a flat no. Too many salespeople lose sales needlessly at this point by translating this to mean no. There is a better way to handle it: Treat it as a request for more information. Here's how:

"Of course, Mr. Thompson. I understand. And to help you make your decision, you might want to consider. . . ." At this point you give him a few more benefits, concluding with a closing question.

Don't forget to keep the name and phone number of those inquiries who don't buy; you will want to follow up on them later. The company may still be a good prospect even though you didn't sell that particular buyer on the phone. Call him back later on. Also, buyer moods and circumstances change—as does personnel.

Use the phone for progress reports as you develop a sale. You must frequently "sell" a number of levels of "buyers," before a final commitment is made. As you move through these different influencers, you need to keep the project alive via regular progress reports to every one of them. Your voice contact sparks good emotional feelings.

Use the Phone to Push
for the Appointment
With "Mr. Right."

Your probing has by now gotten you the name of the *real* decision maker. And you have learned that since these decision makers don't have time to see all salespeople who want to see them, they have come to depend on their various "screens" to evaluate these salespeople, as well as their products or services.

As an exceptional salesperson, you won't be following the flock, taking the usual route through Mr. Right's screens. Don't misunderstand this; screens are fine people—and they keep a lot of your would-be competition away. Since you must work with them, it behooves you to realize how they can either help you or hurt you. Make their job easier and they will make yours easier. Just realize that a screen may be paid to politely say "no" to your proposition. Only Mr. Right can say either "yes" or "no."

By being the exception and getting through to see Mr. Right, you will carry more clout as you talk with others in the company. Also, in a bid situation, you may be the only one who got through to a face-to-face meeting. That personal rapport established with the person at the top can make the difference in getting the business. Of course, this isn't going to happen all the time, but you jump your percentages of getting the bid by trying, even on your very first call!

Once you've begun to work with a screen, you will need to find ways to meet the decision maker without stepping on the screen's toes. We'll cover that in Chapter 11—the closing process.

Here are some "pleasantly pushy" (not obnoxious) methods for getting the appointment with Mr. Right. Let's assume that you have already learned that Mr. Right's secretary is Helen Jones. You have probably discovered by now that when you ask for Mr. Right, you often get somebody who answers with something like this:

"Mr. Right's office. May I help you?"

Now at this point you need to assume that she is going to put you through to her employer. So, with a pleasant but confident voice, you say something like:

"Good morning. Helen Jones? This is Bill Smith, with Blank Company. Is Mr. Right in?"

She may ask you what your call is about, or suggest that you talk with someone else "who takes care of such things." Remaining calm but persistent, your response would be something like this:

"Oh, of course. I plan to see him, also. But I do need to see Mr. Right briefly while I am out there. Is he in now so I can set this up?"

Should you continue to be blocked, try this: "I've got an idea that I need Mr. Right's opinion on and I'm talking about a very brief time—possibly at around 9:45 tomorrow morning. Is he in now, or perhaps you could just set it up for me."

When you get your decision maker on the line, be sure to get your identity across clearly and distinctly. Don't rush. Be friendly but not subservient. Remember, you are important, too! And you have something that will help your prospect or his company. However, Mr. Right may also pass you off to a screen. But, you're prepared for this.

"Fine," you say. "I want to meet Mr. Jacobs. However, while I'm there, I'd like to see you just briefly at, say, about 9:45 in the morning . . ."

Next, use in your own words this highly-productive sentence:

"I've got an idea that can really cut your inventory costs, but I do need your opinion and input on it."

You can substitute whatever "idea" is appropriate to your proposition; that is, "an idea that will drastically reduce maintenance costs . . . an idea that will increase your income."

You might get an answer like, "What idea is that?" Of course, your job is to sell the *appointment*, not the product or service over the phone. You might try something like this in reply:

"It is something graphic that I want to show you . . . and I'm talking about a very brief amount of time, either at 9:45, or possibly at about 3:15 in the afternoon."

Now your "idea" doesn't have to be something spectacular—it could be anything about your product or service. In fact, you *do* need his input. The "graphic"? Your "visual" could be anything you could show your prospect: a picture, a testimonial letter, a graph, or a page in your catalog.

Let's assume your prospect says he's not in the market for whatever you're selling. You have what amounts to a turndown. Try this:

"I can certainly understand that, Mr. Right. It would be presumptuous of me to think I could call you this morning and you would say, 'Yes, come on out. We want to buy some forklift trucks.' Of course not. But I've got an idea, and I do need your input on it . . . I'm talking about a very brief amount of time at about 9:45 in the morning. And, I'd like to meet you." Perhaps this time you will get an answer like:

"Well, 9:45 is all right, but I really don't think we'll be doing anything at this time." You might come back with:

"I understand. I'm putting it on my calendar for 9:45. And my name, again, is . . ."

People forget appointments. You are indirectly triggering an imitation response in him when you mention that you are marking it on your calendar. And, since he may have already forgotten your name, your reminder will probably be appreciated. Another thing this does is show your own self-respect and your businesslike manner.

Of course, the conversation could take another turn. He could refuse you the appointment—simply tell you he isn't interested. Try asking if another day would be better. Suggest another day yourself. Again drop the idea that you need his input on something. It could be that you are just hitting him when he's busy and next week *would* be better. However, if you sense the slightest irritation, pull back. Don't forget the "pleasant" part of being "pleasantly pushy." This should come across in your manner and tone. Of course, it won't work every time, but you will be making many more appointments where they count—at the decision-making level.

In interviews I have conducted with decision makers, I have found that most of them have gotten into certain pet ways to say no! They are accustomed to having salespeople backing off at the least excuse. So they use these excuses over and over again.

Here are some pet excuses and put-offs:

—We just don't have it in the budget right now.
—We're happy with our present supplier.
—Things are a little tight now, maybe later on . . .
—See us after the first of the year.
—Send us a brochure.

In most cases these are simply meaningless, designed to put you off or get rid of you in a nice way. The reason they are used so often is that they work in 98 percent of all cases! They needn't work on you, however. Most decision makers are not accustomed to salespeople who are persistent in a pleasant, intriguing way.

HOW TO USE A "SECRETARY" TO QUALIFY AND SET UP CALLS

There are two ways you can handle this. The calling party can attend only to qualifying the prospect, leaving the setting up of the appointment to the salesperson. When using this method, you would send each qualified prospect a letter explaining that you will be contacting him soon for an appointment. The second method requires that your "secretary" handle the whole thing—qualifying the prospect and setting up the appointment. Much the same techniques are used here, but study the following example:

"Mr. Right? This is Ann Maxwell with the Crighton Company. Don Martin, our district representative, wanted me to call you. He wants very much to see you . . . if possible, this Thursday afternoon about 3:20, or possibly next Monday morning. He's got an idea he wants your opinion on regarding a money-saving packing device. Is 3:20 Thursday all right, or would Monday morning be better?"

Let's assume that the prospect says he's not interested in making any changes now.

"Certainly, I understand. And Mr. Martin asked me to tell you that even if you weren't making any changes, he would like your input on the device . . . and also, he'd like to meet you. Which would be the easiest time for you?"

You may also want to call an hour before any scheduled appointment and confirm it.

Using a mailogram to confirm out of town appointments attracts favorable attention.

Use the Telephone to Sell
and Service Small and Marginal Accounts

It costs somewhere between $2.00 and $5.00 for each sales call made by telephone, including overhead costs. On the other hand, a face-to-face call may run as high as $165.00 or more, according to some sources. Frequent phone calling is the only practical way to handle small customers.

Just remember to choose those methods that are the most practical for you. And work on your telephone technique as an actor would on a stage role. Make sure that you always sound spontaneous, however. Your talk should never sound "canned." Keep good records of calls and mailings.

One more thing: Phone calls shouldn't be made just when you "can find the time." Right at the beginning, block out certain periods of time for making phone calls.

7

How to Read People Accurately

Most sales training centers on product or service knowledge. This is vital, but there is little in-depth training in perception of the true feelings of the prospect. These feelings encompass a wide range of fears and doubts concerning the sales proposition. How do you cope with these feelings and close the sale? How do you read people accurately, then what do you do about the things you perceive? There is one important fact that you must remember as you move into this area.

The words of a prospect actually tell very little about how he feels. We express most of our feelings with the eyes, gestures, and voice. Behavioral studies suggest that only about 7 percent of what we feel is expressed through the use of words. Another 38 percent is expressed through the tone we use—through rate of speaking and speech inflection. Nonverbal factors, expressed through the face and eyes and through gestures, account for 55 percent.

To accurately "read" people, one must get into the habit of catching the quick changes in the eyes and face. These fleeting changes may last only a quarter to a half second! This is especially true of the eyes, with their more direct connection to the brain. If our own eyes are sharp enough, we can perceive the change in pupil size of our prospect's eyes. In expressing keen interest and emotional stimulus, the pupils can increase in size as much as 30 percent. There are some professional card sharks who can see these changes. For instance, a player could keep a "poker face," but there's no way to keep the pupils from changing if he were to draw a royal flush.

Even though you may not have this kind of perception, you can easily see the changing expressions of the eyes. Accurately reading these changes, however, is largely habit. Practice observing changes in the eyes. Start with the first person you talk to when you put this book down.

There are many muscles around the eyes. The brain is giving these muscles messages such as, "You make me feel good, and for that I like you," (The eyes seem to brighten as the muscles change the shape.) Or the brain may tell the muscles, "I wish this guy would hurry up; I'm not that interested in this deal, but I don't want to hurt his feelings." (The muscles give the eyes a hanging, dull look. The muscles in the face hang, giving way occasionally to a half-hearted smile in response to the directive not to hurt the person's feelings.) Frequently, a person is looking right at you, perhaps even with a pleasant expression. You think he is listening. But something is taking place in the brain about whether or not to call Mary tonight. The message to the muscles around the eyes change, and the eyes take on a slightly different look that say, "Sorry, I'm thinking about something else right now."

A prospect is flashing true messages to us every moment; all we have to do is read them. We've all been reading people, whether we realize it or not since we were toddlers. But for top performance in selling, we need to bring this perception to a conscious level. To accurately "read" the prospect, we must be acutely aware of his interests and feelings at all times. Emotions and interests are there for us to read in the body language and in the voice changes. The decision to buy is emotional; facts and logic simply back up the emotional decision. This also applies to routine industrial buying of products and services.

In reading body language, it isn't necessary for us to memorize a hundred gestures and their interpretations. If we tried to do this, we would be wrong much of the time. For example, a person with folded arms might be expressing rejection; but the person might also be cold or just comfortable in that position. Another problem with trying to keep track of too many gestures is that our concentration would be totally taken up by analyzing the prospect rather than concerned with closing the sale. Fortunately, there is an easier and more accurate way: We need to be aware of five body language "clusters."

Total Rejection

We don't get total rejection very often, but when it comes we need to know what to do with it. Certainly, you can't close until you change rejection into acceptance. The arms might be folded: That wouldn't tell you much unless you also noticed a clinched fist or a touching of the side of the nose. Other important signals are shoulders at an angle to you (very important), tight lips, eyes cold—possibly drifting away from yours. If standing, the person may back away. His voice is rather flat and he probably gives short answers.

What do you do? *Stop selling!* Then do something that may seem a bit gutsy—ask why you are being rejected. Maybe not in those words, but do something like this: Pause. If you're holding a pen, slowly put it down on the desk. Then lightly, with a smile, say something like, "Mr. Chadwick, I've got a feeling this just doesn't interest you. Is it me, or the presentation, or did I just catch you at a bad time?" *Repeat: This must be done in a warm, light manner.* What will happen? You have just separated yourself from the pack. You will have raised yourself in the eyes of the prospect. You haven't insulted him; you have shown *empathy*!

You'll get some strange answers. (No, the prospect isn't going to say that the problem is you. And even if he did, you would learn something.) One answer I'll never forget was that of a developer in Dallas. He was the executive vice-president of the firm. He didn't answer me right away, but he soon looked straight at me and said, "Mr. Patton, we're going bankrupt!" An hour earlier he had learned the fate of his company. Actually, I wasn't being rejected; the man was in a mild state of shock. On other occasions where I've used that sentence, the rejections turned immediately into sales.

Let's say that you have a two o'clock appointment. You come in smiling. However, your prospect has just had a disagreeable conversation with someone—perhaps his boss. He's mad; his ego's been hurt. So he's probably preoccupied as you go through your presentation. He's showing rejection. You say, lightly, "I have a feeling this just isn't interesting you. Is it me, or what I'm showing you, or did I just catch you at a bad time?"

Practice using that gutsy little sentence. Do it your own way, in your own natural manner. Phrase the words as you like; just be sure it's light and warm. Then stand in front of a mirror and rehearse it. Professional actors spend hours in front of a mirror practicing every gesture, every "off-handed" remark. The top people in any field rehearse. It's practice . . . practice . . . practice.

Using this technique, you will have prospects apologize, as has happened to me, then turn right around, pay rapt attention— and buy! Certainly, not always—but it happens.

Indifference

This attitude is common. It's particularly common where buyers are seeing many salespeople every day. Some of them seem to say to themselves, as the next salesperson is shuttled in, "OK, turkey, so tell me why *your* product is number one in the industry." And this is understandable. They have to sit through many insufferably boring presentations. After many years of this, they just don't get all that excited when another salesperson walks in the door.

I like to call this cluster the "hangs." When a person is bored or indifferent, the muscles of the face literally hang. A person looks 10 years older with the hangs. You've seen it in restaurants; two people eating, not conversing, the muscles on their faces drooping. If the prospect shows this, you'll probably also notice a haggard look around his eyes. He may squirm occasionally in the chair, or tap the desk, or lean back with his hands behind his neck. There may be little response to your questions. If standing, the prospect probably won't get too close. Any two or three of these would be a "cluster," and your diagnosis would likely be accurate.

What do you do? Again, *stop selling*. Use the same technique as you would with the rejection. Here's why. You'll immediately get the person's undivided attention. Here, too, you will raise the buyer's opinion of you (provided it is done warmly, lightly, and sincerely). You will also get the real objections rather than disinterest or boredom.

In interviews I've had with prospects and decision makers, I've learned an interesting fact: Many do not want to give you an objection. The reason is they know you'll probably come up with some answers you've already prepared. They don't want to take the time to hear them. They may be obligated, or at least feel that they are obligated, to see salespeople. So they wait for the salesperson to come to the end of the presentation before they offer some stock answer such as, "Why don't you leave me your brochure." It's a nice way of winding up a sales interview. The salesperson can put something down on the call report and the prospect puts the brochure aside (in the wastebasket or in his files).

You can't afford this kind of treatment; you've spent time and money to get to this spot in front of the prospect, and you don't need indifference. If there are objections, you need to know exactly what they are. To get at these you must draw out the prospect. Objections aren't to be dreaded—indifference is. Objections are opportunities; they give you the fuel to carry your presentation to a closing. How to handle objections will follow later.

Lying

Following gestures isn't 100 percent accurate, but the percentage of accuracy is high. Suppose a person you are talking to says something like, "We just don't have it in the budget." At the same time a hand goes up to the face. The person may squirm in his chair, or, if standing, shift his weight. The eyes will usually turn away or down from yours. Your perception that the prospect's statements are not true is probably correct.

Confusion

In the middle of your presentation, you may perceive a slight scowl, a pursing of the mouth, or perhaps a puzzled look. Quite possibly you have said something that the prospect does not understand. Remember the ego—nobody wants to appear stupid. I have seen this cluster many times as I sat in on sales presentations. In one case, a real estate salesperson was explaining a method of purchasing and said, "We could use a 'wrap-around' contract." Men like to think of themselves as knowledgeable in finance and contracts. Or, at least, that's the image they're supposed to project. In this case, the prospect just scowled and said, "Well, let me think about it."

     I've seen it frequently in the high-tech business. The computer business is full of buzz words: menu, modem, RAM and ROM, buffer, hard disc and floppy disc. And as these words are being glibly tossed out, what's the prospect to do when he doesn't know what they mean? Asking may make him feel stupid, so he doesn't buy . . . or . . . he gets hold of a salesperson who explains clearly, who builds his ego, who paints the benefits of how he'll enjoy his new computer.

     Remember this: If a person is not *completely* clear about what you are offering, he will not buy. Prospects will say, "Let me think about it," or, "I don't believe I'm interested." *Everything* you present—features, benefits, terms, cost, delivery, installation, warranty—must be crystal clear and simple to understand.

     What do you do when you get the "confusion" cluster? Back up and go over what you have said; say it in a different way. Say something like, "Let me summarize it" or "Let me go over that again." Sometimes, what appears to be the body language of confusion isn't confusion at all, but doubt; doubt about benefits or doubt about cost justification. You must probe to bring out the prospect's real feelings.

Interest

The prospect might show a liking toward you or what you're saying, or both. He may start with a mildly interested look, perhaps leaning back in his chair. As interest grows, he may lean forward and face you directly. Eyes seem to sparkle and show animation, and the prospect looks at you frequently. If you're both standing, he may move closer. His voice sounds interested and he responds easily to your questions. He may even nod his head.

You're getting buying signals. It's time to close. Closing takes many shapes; you may have to close an engineer before you can close the VP of production. Similarly, you may have to close the wife and then the husband. You may have to sell the president, and then convince his accountant or tax attorney. In many cases, selling is actually a series of closes.

We're going to get into closing techniques, closing a group, and negotiating the close in chapters that follow. But right now, let's examine how you might respond to this "interest cluster." Depending on the situation, you could turn to one of the various techniques suggested in Chapter 11 on closing, or you could simply get a commitment on some point. You do this by offering a choice.

The "choice" might go something like this; "Mr. Snyder, let me ask you . . . of these two plans, which do you think would be best for your purposes?" He might say, "Well, I like this plan best because of those three tax shelters and the comparative safety of the investment." And you could come back with, "All right, why don't I detail the complete plan and. . . ." You are into the close!

Suppose he says he wants to think it over? You might reply, "I can understand that. Certainly! Careful thought should go into this. But at this point, which of the two plans appeal to you most?" He might respond, "Probably this plan, but—like I said—I want to give it some thought."

"I understand," you say. "Now there are two ways that this can be set up . . ." And you continue getting commitments on certain points. You may be able to get enough of those commitments to where the stall of "thinking it over" is forgotten. Then again, you may have to make another call on the prospect. However, drawing the prospect out to the commitments has helped focus his attention on benefits, in addition to giving you insight on how to proceed on the follow-up call. Do take notes as you discuss the various points. It gives you an "assumptive" posture. You expect that he is going to buy. The assumptive close is one of the most powerful and effective tools you can use.

HOW TO "FOCUS" LISTEN

Look for the "cluster" areas on all your calls. This will give you a track to run on as you proceed. Listen for these clusters, too.

If you took all the tools of selling and selected one as the most valuable, I believe that the ability to *listen* would be number one! The top salesman with one of our largest insurance companies was asked why, in his opinion, he had become his company's top salesperson.

"Because I listen," was his instant response. "And after I've been listening for awhile, people seem to warm up. Then they listen as I discuss their problems and the things that they want in life. I make a few suggestions and the business comes naturally."

What I'm talking about is focus listening: *observant* listening. This is difficult because we think at the rate of about 400 to 700 words a minute, while the prospect may be talking at only 100 to 130 words a minute. Our attention is apt to drift. Also, we are too often preoccupied with ourselves —we're thinking about what we're going to say next. Or we are distracted by what we see and it takes great effort to concentrate.

But one of the biggest problems is that most people think they listen well. Listening occupies the largest part of all our communicating time—about 45 percent. It is important, therefore, that we learn to listen well. This great sales tool isn't all that easy to come by, but the habit can be developed by using the following method for just five days. Follow this plan and notice how it raises your concentration level. Also, notice how much more interesting you are to others! Focus listening is charismatic. It sells!

Simply practice these four key points for 30 minutes a day, beginning now:

1. Face the person.
2. Listen actively by nodding and saying such things as "I see" and "Really?"
3. Get pupil contact. You don't have to stare your prospect down, but have *some* contact.
4. Hang on every word. This sounds a lot easier than it is. We all dart around in our thinking. We pick up a word or two, then off we go into our own little world as the prospect continues to talk. Perhaps we notice something about his teeth, or hair, or clothing.

During your 30-minute practice sessions, try to really concentrate and hold your attention span for as long as you can. You will still be distracted, but you will notice that your attention level improves each day.

You may wonder why I suggest practicing for only 30 minutes each day instead of all day long. I've worked with many people in this experiment and have noticed that when they try to do it all day long, they soon forget about it. Several days later they remember to try it again for a few minutes. They are never able to capture the idea and make a habit of it. But by disciplining themselves for just 30 minutes a day, many of these people could take hold of the idea and stay with it for an entire week. Those who did reported that their listening habits were improved. One point: Try to make it the same hour of the day each day. On a few of those times you may find somebody really boring: Use this opportunity to test your new skills in concentration.

As you do this, you will notice that your powers of perception are increasing. You'll be reading people more accurately and you'll pick up on their true feelings. And, of course, you'll be a much more interesting person.

Selling is such a complex interchange with people that you sometimes wonder if you are doing the right things. Frequently, it's a blend of common sense, intuition, and perception. We'll cover a number of these "what to do" situations in the chapters that follow.

8

The Critical
First Three Minutes

You are actually into the close within the first three minutes with a prospect! The outcome of your presentation is frequently determined in those first 180 seconds.

Consider the way you buy a book or magazine. That cover is doing most of the selling. It's appealing strongly to your emotions. Colors, type, and design must bite with emotional appeal. Article titles are "you" oriented—how to help *you* get what *you* want. You pick it up, take a couple seconds to skim a few pages, or take a closer glance at those subheads. Now you will make the decision to buy or not to buy. What you saw in those few moments must lock onto what your ego *wants*. In those moments your emotions must build the believability that you need it. Or maybe the desire is stimulated to first scan it a bit more until you actually *feel* that it is worth your money.

In the same manner, the prospect's computer mind is taking you in. "Like" or "dislike" is going on in the prospect's subconscious mind. There's a feeling there either of wanting or not wanting to do business with you. And all this happens even before you give your presentation. During these initial moments, the prospect may not appear judgmental at all. But inside, his brain is making computer-like computations at a terrific rate. Feelings about you are being quickly formed; likes and dislikes are being tallied—they include your hair, your hands and fingernails, your body, your clothing, your skin, your teeth, your lips, eyes, and nose. An estimate is made of your self-confidence and poise, your age and sex, your carriage and mannerisms, the way you sit, your eye contact, the touch of your handshake, your smile, your neatness and cleanliness, your voice influence and choice of words, your apparent intelligence, and, most importantly, your attitude and expression of interest, caring, warmth, and spontaneity.

To find out more of what happens in that critical first three minutes, we did extensive video taping of the initial approach of a number of salespeople. Twelve areas of evaluation were used. In creating favorable impressions, sometimes just a few major qualities can count heavily. You'll probably feel secure about yourself in most of these areas; however, if an item, word, or sentence brings forth a momentary twinge of doubt about yourself, then stop and ask yourself, "Can I possibly improve on this?"

TRYING TOO HARD TO IMPRESS CAN HAVE A NEGATIVE EFFECT   You can become so engrossed in making a good impression that it comes across as insincere, "put on," or shallow. One's very dress could come across as too self-concerned. It would be self-defeating to be so overly concerned with impression and appearance that the wonderful qualities of warmth, caring, and being yourself don't come through.

A WARM SMILE SAYS "I LIKE YOU"   Some anxiety in those first three minutes is good. The adrenalin is pumping, you're mentally alert. But if there's too much anxiety, there may be a forced, tense smile, or maybe a nervous laugh. A smile that is warm and genuine says "I like you, I'm interested in you." It's also saying "I feel good about myself and about life." That kind of smile dissolves tension between you and your prospect. It puts aside negative feelings and prejudice. It opens the door to your own flow of positive, constructive ideas.

Such a smile doesn't start on the lips—it comes from inside of you; it's the physical manifestation of an attitude. The great thing about it is that you can actually program the attitude into your mind. It's all a matter of self-conditioning or psyching yourself up, as the athletes say. They use this strategy in the locker room and on the field. Many sports greats and near-greats have spent hours alone before an event, programming winning attitudes into the subconscious.

PROGRAM YOUR MIND ON THE WAY TO EACH CALL   This can make the difference of whether your smile is flat or tense, or warm and engaging. Aloud, in the car, simply say, "She and I will have great rapport. We'll get along great." Yes, say it aloud. Of course, if you're in an office or store and others are around you, saying this aloud will make others wonder about you. But you can still say it quietly to your-self. Practice this kind of programming, even if you feel relaxed about the call. Your subconscious mind will be absorbing it.

Be aware, however, that this won't work if, at the same time, you have feelings of dislike toward the prospect. Your very movements will reflect this feeling when you meet. Also, do not say, "I'm going to sell her today." If you do this, negative feedback will creep in, and you will almost hear it whisper, "No, you won't." What you really want to do is to program in the feeling, "I care about this person. I will find ways to help this person. We will get along great." This is true positive thinking. It is highly effective mind programming.

I was riding with a distributor salesman once, and I asked, "Where are we going next?"

"Oh, we've got to make a call on a real horse's _____ (exple-tive). Can't stand the guy," was the salesman's reply. We made the call. They smiled at each other, but nothing happened. When we got back in the car I asked my friend, "You didn't really expect to sell him, did you?"

"Why do you say that?" he asked.

"Because of the way you feel about him."

"Oh, he doesn't know I feel that way about him," he said.

"The heck he doesn't," I said. "There's something to this thing about 'vibes.' People subconsciously pick up on the way we feel about them . . . and return those feelings. Next time, think of something good about the man." He gave me a serious look.

"But there's nothing good about him," he said.

During the handshake, more than half of all salespeople let their eyes look down or away from a prospect's eyes. This is an uncon-scious habit of many people. It's hard to know whether you do this or not. So, do some thinking about this beforehand. Plan to make excellent *pupil contact* with the prospect and to hold the gaze for a few seconds. Plan to lock onto those pupils even if you feel uncomfortable and want to look away. Now, I'm not talking about staring anyone down—that would be uncomfortable and rude. I'm talking about getting and show-ing control and self-confidence. A salesperson may have all the self-confidence in the world, but by not meeting the eye, it appears that he or she lacks it. And it's not good enough just to look at the prospect's eyes: You travel from the pupil, to the eyes, to the face.

An excellent way to find out whether or not you're making pupil contact is to ask yourself after the call, "What color eyes does she have?'' If you can name the color, you have made excellent pupil contact. Ask yourself that question following all your calls for the next three days. It will help you to form the habit.

PUT THAT HAND OUT   This applies to both sexes. Some men are tentative about extending their hand first to a woman. The old school says the woman should extend her hand first, or withhold it, as she chooses. Times have changed. Both salesmen and saleswomen should extend their hand. People enjoy the gesture—some are shy and really appreciate your taking the initiative. Salesmen should give a firm full grip to a woman, not taking the ends of the fingers as though she were fragile. That's a bit macho, a throwback to the days when men kissed the back of a woman's hand. A handshake should be firm, obviously not limp nor too hard. A too-hard handshake tells the prospect that the salesman doesn't have confidence but is trying to come across like he has an abundance of it.

YOUR SPONTANEITY SETS THE RIGHT STAGE   Everything about you in those first moments sets the tone of the meeting. If you are tense, your prospect may become tense without realizing it. If you are very serious, your prospect will usually become serious. It is the same situation when a speaker steps to the podium.

The speaker tries to set the right mood; so should you. In selling, you're after a relaxed, warm, receptive atmosphere. One of the best ways to do this is to be totally open in those first seconds when you and your prospect meet. People admire, like, trust—and respond to—openness. You say pretty much what comes to mind at the moment—you are spontaneous; you are emotional. Since you've already programmed your attitude, you know that your smile is warm, that your spontaniety won't include a tirade of negatives. Actually, you'll find that as you get in the habit of "programming" your attitude before each call, your level of spontaneity goes way up. Call it openness, naturalness, enthusiasm, charisma; it does the job and it sets the stage for a smooth closing.

THE "SQUEAKY CLEAN" LOOK REFRESHES OTHERS   A shampoo ad talks about hair that feels "squeaky clean." And it's great to feel that way. For salespeople it's a *must* that they look that way—it's the look of success. Perhaps some people can get away with being a bit careless now and then, but for a salesperson, it's got to be 100 percent clean. That means no trace of dandruff, no missing button, no small spot or small run—not even a few scuff marks on your shoes. And it means carrying breath mints to be on the safe side. Teeth must be clean, with no dark cavities or missing teeth.

One day a very warm salesman came to see me about buying an accounting system. When he smiled, there was an empty space toward the back of his mouth when a molar should have been. Yet, he was wearing a Rolex watch! I'll frequently see people displaying expensive jewelry while their teeth are crying for attention. When needed, capping, filing, and bridgework are some of the best investments a salesperson can make.

WHEN YOU BUY CLOTHES, BUY QUALITY   If you have a limited budget for clothing, it's better to buy just a few clothes of top quality rather than a large variety of poor quality. Clothes on the bargain rack or table sometimes look good—until the first washing or cleaning. Go with the style that looks good on you rather than just going with the latest fad. Some designers' fashions do absolutely nothing for a woman. Some magazine articles have suggested that women wear severe cuts in order to look assertive. I know a number of very graciously assertive women executives and top saleswomen who do very well looking feminine.

A word of caution: A saleswoman should not look too sexy. If she's calling on men, other men in the same office may kid her prospect. It may sound ridiculous, but the prospect may be afraid to buy for fear of what other men may say or think. If the real estate woman looks or acts too sexy, this could be a detriment to helping a couple find a home. The wife may be paying more attention to the sudden "happy" mood of her husband.

How you dress depends a lot on who you call on. Certainly, if you're calling on ad agencies, you may choose to wear the latest style. And if you're a man calling on maintenance engineers and you show up in a special pants design right out of New Yorker Magazine, you may not get the rapport you want. If you're selling drilling mud and you make calls on toolpushers at the rig site, you'd look ridiculous in a suit. However, if part of the day is spent with men in offices, you should dress accordingly, probably leaving your coat in the car when you're at a drilling site.

Your appearance is part of the overall package that you sell. Just as advertising creates a specific image for a product, you should do the same for yourself. That means the right appearance, even when you don't expect to see anyone.

One day in a real estate office, I noticed that one of the women had a bandana on her head. She was doing some phone work and didn't have any showings that afternoon. But she wasn't building her image with others in the office. It does make a difference. Good appearance boosts the respect and the help you receive from others. Psychological tests have proved this. Not only that, it boosts one's own alertness and enthusiasm. Tests conducted among people attending seminars and sales meetings have demonstrated this. The groups that were better dressed absorbed more!

LET SILENCE WORK FOR YOU   Sometimes there is an awkward silence just after the greeting and handshake. It is a period of not knowing what to say next. Here's something that may help: Silence is actually a wonderful selling tool. We are all so used to turning on the radio or TV that, for the most part, we can't tolerate silence. That's what gives it its power—provided it's *controlled* silence. And provided you don't feel embarrassed or at a loss for words. With a few seconds of controlled silence just after the greeting, your strength, confidence, and control are felt. You're not rambling just to fill space. Instead of dreading silence, you can start using it to your advantage.

USE SMALL TALK TO GET A GOOD "HOOK-UP" WITH YOUR PROSPECT   When two humans interact with each other, they are looking for bonds of sameness. We feel comfortable with others who are like us; we feel stiff and uneasy with those who are different from us. We want approval from others and we question whether the approval is there when we're with people who seem different from us.

Small talk bridges differences. It makes us feel closer to the other person. In selling, the more comradery we have with others, the more we sell. However, if our small talk sounds contrived or phony, it does not bring us closer—it may do just the opposite. Some purchasing agents have a lot of fun with this. I know one who bought a racing-car trophy and had it displayed on his desk just to see what opening remarks he could evoke. Another very heavy fellow looks for reactions to a sleek diving trophy. This is not intended to suggest that if you see a trophy in a prospect's office and you are honestly impressed by it, that you shouldn't comment on it. Sincerity is the guide.

"How's business?" isn't one of the best small-talk openers. Use it and you're sure to get some negative responses and, hence, a built-in reason for not buying. Be observant as you approach your prospect; this may give you a good opener. However, if you find yourself with absolutely nothing to say, don't force the small talk. It's better in this instance to simply smile and begin to explain exactly why you are there. Here are a few ideas that can help you to use small talk effectively.

After you're seated, you could say something like, "Mr. Jones, I'm certainly glad we could get together this afternoon. I've been looking forward to this." This is strictly small talk, a bit of hook-up before you get down to business. Again, put something like that into your own words. And don't even attempt it if you don't mean it. If you can find something about which you naturally have mutual interests—sport interests, children of the same age, common backgrounds—all of these can bridge the "stranger gap."

BE SURE EVERYTHING ABOUT YOU IS SAYING NICE THINGS Generally, you sit forward a bit in your chair, but don't slouch. And remember, the prospect's desk is private property. If you put anything on it, such as a briefcase, flipchart, or audio-visual instrument, be certain that you're not putting it on some of the prospect's papers. He might be concerned about your creasing or otherwise damaging his papers. When you write anything, use an attractive gold pen, not a freebie plastic advertising pen.

Your notebooks, catalogs, and presentation books should all be neat and attractive. No loose sheets should hang or fall out. Your briefcase should have a neat, efficient, and professional look. If you are not the efficient type, just make up your mind to at least *look* like you are. Every weekend, reorganize your materials: Discard all the junk, and restructure the contents.

Present your business card as soon as you sit down. In five minutes, the prospect may have forgotten your name, and if he thinks he might have to introduce you to someone else, he'll be worrying about your name rather than listening to you. Present the card on the second and third call you make on this prospect, too. Remember that your prospect may be seeing 10 or 20 salespeople a day.

GET THERE AT LEAST FIVE MINUTES EARLY   Instead of rushing in to make the appointment, use the extra few minutes to observe things that you can use in the interview. Here are some things you'll want to check on:

1. The "pecking order" of parking spaces. There may be names of people you should know on some of those spaces.
2. Boxes being loaded or unloaded. Check physical size of the business and employee parking area.
3. Look over plaques and trade journals in the lobby. See if your prospect's company has an ad in the trade journals. Listen for names and conversations; pick up brochures and annual reports. Ask the receptionist questions. Leaf through the guest register to see if your competitor has been there and who his contact was. Possibly you can obtain a corporate chart from the receptionist.

If you get caught in traffic and you feel that you might be even a minute late, it's better to pull off and make a telephone call. Some prospects are sticklers about salespeople being on time. With some, being even a minute late can prejudice your case. Also, do check with the recep-tionist in a polite way to be sure that your prospect knows you are there.

DO A PRE-CALL CHECKLIST ON THE WAY TO EVERY CALL   Do this, and watch the results! Pilots do it. They wouldn't think of taking off without running down a checklist. You should do this on every sales call. It takes about two minutes. See how much more in control you are using this checklist; watch how it guides the meeting right into the close. And it's so simple. Just type out the following checklist and put it on the sunvisor of your car (or anywhere else it'll be easy to refer to as you drive). On your way to each call, go through these 15 points:

The Pre-Call Checklist
1.   Am I seeing the decision maker? (If not, how can I get to the decision maker?)
2.   What are his probable personal goals?
3.   How can I help him with these goals?
4.   How can I help him look good to others?
5.   What are his company's goals?
6.   How will what I sell help him achieve these goals?
7.   Who might be the "influencers" in getting a favorable decision?
8.   What three benefits will I present?
9.   What features back these up?
10.   To show proof, what testimonial stories can I use?
11.   What visuals will I use?
12.   What competition am I up against?
13.   What are my strengths?
14.   What objections will probably be brought up or hidden?
15.   What action do I want on this call?

Before you get to the interview, say those key words, buzzwords, and letter groupings *seven times*. There seems to be some psychological magic in repeating something seven times. Use this technique and your closings will be more effective immediately! Every industry has certain words that should flow easily in your talk. Some examples are OEM (original equipment manufacturer), CPM (cost per thousand, in adver-tising), demographics (age, income, sex race). Many companies have some of their own. Learn them and repeat them aloud as you are driving. Repeat 7 times exact product names, the company name, and the names of people you will be talking to.

You will want to thread names and any expressions into your presentation. Of course, you must know exactly what an expression means or you'll sound like a fool. But learn to use them correctly and notice the increased attention value of your presentation. Really learn them, and they will come out in your presentation without a hesitation or a falter.

The LASAR Technique
for Remembering Names

I was going down the aisle in a supermarket one day with my wife, Nelle. Suddenly I bumped right into one of my customers. My mind went blank—I couldn't think of his name. As we went through the initial pleasantries, Nelle quickly picked up on the delay in the introduction and introduced herself.

Another time I was calling on the president of a company to sell him my sales training program. We were about to leave his office to have lunch and to discuss the program when he suggested we include two of his vice presidents. I certainly agreed. He called them into his office and I was introduced. Somehow, the names went right by me. As we went down the elevator, I realized I needed to get their names right, but figured I'd pick up on them later.

We drove to the restaurant, and after the meal I went into some of the presentaion. An old friend of mine was also in the restaurant. He spotted me, and came over to say hello. He and I chatted in a friendly way as I tried to pretend that my failure to introduce him was simply an oversight. Finally, as he smiled at them, they introduced themselves. I didn't fool anyone.

After that last embarrassing incident, I decided to find a sure-fire method for remembering names. I studied various techniques. Many of these methods covered getting the name right and repeating it. There are a number of excellent methods using the memory peg and association idea. Such methods actually date back to Caesar's time. Some were too involved. I wanted something simple ... something that really works, easily and quickly. To begin with, I reasoned that I had to find out why we forget names.

WHY WE FORGET NAMES

The key reason we forget names is that we don't care! That is the blunt truth of the matter. There's nothing wrong with our memory; we're just not motivated enough to remember.

During an introduction, if the person's name is said too quickly or is slurred, we will usually just let it go. Most of the time, we just don't care that much about it. We aren't interested enough to ask that the name be repeated. Sometimes, during an introduction, we are preoccupied with other thoughts. Maybe we are too concerned with ourselves and worry about the kind of impression we make on others. When that happens, we pay very little attention to the other person's name. And even if we get the name right, we usually don't care enough to make the effort of repeating it—much less bothering to write it down.

We Are
Distracted Visually

Our sense of sight is by far the strongest. During an introduction, our mind is gathering data such as the approximate age of the person, the look of his or her skin, the whiteness and evenness of the teeth, the set of the eyes, the cut of the clothes. With all that visual data coming in, we tend to ignore much of what we hear. And that includes the person's name. Even if we caught the name, the retention level might be fleeting. Studies show that 85 percent of our learning is visual, and that only 11 percent of our learning comes from what we hear. Furthermore, researchers say as much as 80 percent of what we hear is forgotten within just 18 seconds!

"See" the Name

The LASAR techniques will help you to discipline yourself to remember. You will learn a method to enable you to "see" the name and remember it. This system makes catching and recalling names habitual. You'll remember those names in your contact clusters at each follow-up call. Even further, if you wish, you can call people by name as you pass their desks on the way to your key contact. You will be able to do this even if you haven't been there in a month. What an impression! Your competition will still be using that tired old greeting, "Hey, how's it going," while you will be calling everybody by name.

Before learning this technique, try this simple test. A list of names and faces of some well-known professional speakers follows. Look at the pictures and names and pretend you are being introduced to the speakers. Write down as many names as you can remember in the space provided. Refer again to the list and see how many you got. Give yourself a point for each complete name you remember; if you get only the first name or the second name, count it as half a point. Later we'll do another series of pictures using the LASAR technique. You will be pleasantly surprised at the difference in your ability to remember names after applying the LASAR method.

HOW TO REMEMBER NAMES

Desire

In order to remember names and faces, you must first have the desire to do so. But if you don't have this desire, how can you create it? On the one hand, you want to be able to recall names quickly, but on the other hand you don't care that much about a particular individual's name. What do you do? The answer lies in your skill at self-motivation. Perhaps this self-motivation will come easier to you once you realize what a simple method is available to you.

Unless you have had some actual brain damage through an accident, you are using only a small portion of your memorizing ability. Many scientists believe that we may use very little of our brain's potential. Yet, the full capacity to remember thousands of names and faces quickly is right in your skull, *now*! At the height of his political career, the late James Farley was reputed to be able to call 50,000 people by name.

When you call people by name you are using one of the most powerful tools of persuasion . . . and of closing sales. Think for a moment about your own business and social acquaintances. Now think of those casual acquaintances that you really like. Aren't *they* the ones who most quickly and easily call *you* by name?

The ability to remember names is certainly one of the most profitable tools in the psychology of closing sales. Master this skill and you will be miles ahead of your competition. You will stand out among salespeople everywhere you call. Taking the trouble to remember names shows that you care—it creates warmth and goodwill. People will remember *you* because you remember *them*. They see you as an exceptional salesperson because you have made them feel important.

1. John Shults   2. Zig Ziglar   3. John Wolfe   4. Don Thoren

5. Walter Roberson   6. Bill Gove   7. Patricia Fripp   8. "Doc" Blakely

9. Michael Cast   10. Larry Wilson   11. Mort Utley   12. Nicole Schapiro

13. Neal Shaw   14. Naomi Rhodes   15. Bert Decker   16. Bill McGrane, III

17. "Nick" Carter   18. Edwin Bliss   19. Ira Hayes   20. Dottie Walters

1.

2.

3.

4.

5.

6.

7.

8.

9.

10.

11.

12.

13.

14.

15.

16.

17.

18.

19.

20.

76

GET THE "INFLUENCERS" ON YOUR SIDE BY REMEMBERING THEIR NAMES   You will meet a number of influencers as you go about the job of selling, and you will need to have these people on your side. An influencer may be a secretary, a receptionist, a technician, a clerk, a department head, an accountant, an assistant, somebody in marketing or in production, an engineer, an architect, a lawyer, or someone on the administrative staff. An influencer may be the spouse of your client—or it may be a child, relative, or simply a friend.

Whoever the influencers are, the surest way to get them on your side is to call them by name whenever you see them. The little extra trouble it takes you to learn the LASAR technique will enable you to do this and will put you far ahead of the competition. And once you've learned the system, you will be able to "work" it immediately.

Start With the Names
of Business Contacts

You will eventually want to extend your ability so that you will remember the names of almost everybody you meet. But for now, concentrating on business acquaintances should help to assure that you will have the motivation you need to follow through. Since we're talking about increasing your income, that should be enough motivation! Before getting into the LASAR system itself, begin at once to affirm that you *can*, right now, remember names and faces. Never again say anything like "I can remember faces, but I have a hard time with names." Anytime you say something like that you are reprogramming your personal bio-computer. Instead, this very minute, begin to program that computer with this powerful affirmation:

"TODAY I REMEMBER NAMES EASILY."

You will be well started down the road to self-motivation if you repeat this affirmation at least once every day for 30 days.

USING THE LASAR TECHNIQUE
FOR REMEMBERING NAMES

I have found that doing five things in a definite sequence during the first few seconds you are in a person's presence helps to "lock in" the name. The name LASAR is an acronym for this five-step process. Remember these words: Look, Absorb, See, Attach, Repeat. Let's consider them one at a time.

LOOK   In the first few seconds of an introduction, really *look* at the person. Get some pupil contact. You'll also get such visual input as sex, age, and so on.

ABSORB   The instant you hear the name, make a conscious effort to really hear it . . . to *absorb it*. Right after you hear the name, think *absorb*, feel *absorb*. Since you have to do this consciously at the start, there will be times when you forget to think and feel *absorb*. Your desire and effort will quickly establish this as a habit, however. Soon you will reach the point when the second the name is mentioned you will feel that you have absorbed it. Of course, you will no longer be able to let the name slide if you don't get it right. Your commitment to this process means that you will always ask a person to repeat the name if you didn't hear it when first spoken.

SEE   In this step you make it a point to *see* some specific part of the face that strikes you as unique. You see the hair, its color and texture—how far down (or up) it comes on the scalp. You see any bags under the eyes, and observe a wide mouth, large nose, heavy brows, mustache or beard, scars, moles, warts. You see straight or crooked teeth. All of this takes place in an instant, although you will apply it more consciously and more slowly in the beginning. Soon the method takes over and you are doing it subconsciously. As you master the system, your mind will no longer drift away as you look, absorb, and see.

ATTACH   In this step you create an imaginary object which you will use to represent the person's first name. The more weird or unusual the "thing" is, the easier it will be to remember. Next, you mentally attach this object to the person's hair.

You will probably create things different from mine, but here are some of the symbols that I create for this purpose. My "things" are only suggestions—whatever things come easiest to you are what you should use.

Suppose the person's first name is "John." I imagine a six-inch, porcelain "john" sitting in the person's hair. It's important that you put that "john" in the hair. If there is an unusual hairline, that's where you should put the john. Or, if there is wavy, blonde hair, it will sit on one of the waves.

For the name "Mike," I would see a small microphone—a "mike"—in the subject's hair. Try to really see the microphone clearly as you mentally attach a mike to the person's hair.

For "William (Bill)" I "see" a dollar bill rolled up and tucked into some particular feature of the hair. If the person were bald, I'd see the bill pasted down over the bald area.

For "Tom," I'll see a couple of tom-toms in the hair. "Bob" would suggest a small bobcat clawing the hair. For "Jack," a tire jack; for "Henry," an O'Henry candy bar. For "Dennis," I'd put the cartoon character "Dennis The Menace" in the hair. The name "Gary" suggests to me the petro-chemical cracking towers I saw in Gary, Indiana. To you the name "Gary" would probably bring an altogether different picture. What the word pictures to you is what's important.

Is this system infallible? No. I remember one time when I really blew it. I was in the middle of a seminar, demonstrating my ability to introduce about 50 people whom I had just met. I came to one man and introduced him as "Dick." He immediately corrected me and said, "My name's Peter." The group fell apart. They suddenly knew how I was able to remember so many names. You will make mistakes, too, from time to time. But you will still be way ahead in your ability to remember names and faces, in spite of the few mistakes you'll make.

Associations

Many names cannot be represented by a concrete object. When that happens, you can use a representation of some other person who has that same name. Suppose you are introduced to a woman by the name of "Carol." Instantly, your mind gives you the image of another "Carol," perhaps one you knew in grade school. Or you may use one of the famous "Carols"—perhaps Carol Burnette or Carol Channing. Try to see this person in your imagination. Make her about six inches high. See her doing something in your subject's hair—maybe holding a strand of hair, scratching the scalp, or dancing up and down. You will use the same "Carol" more than once, but each time the "Carol" will do something different, according to whose hair she is in.

To illustrate this method further, read this list of names:

Carl	Steve
Ellen	Melissa
Leslie	Mary
Jennifer	Harold
Alice	Craig
Edward	Ann
Gail	

As you say each name, the first name that comes to mind from your past is the one you will want to associate with the current name. Your subject's name is Carl: You picture a Carl you know, dancing in the new

Carl's hair. Or you see an old Ellen pulling your new Ellen's hair or scratching her scalp.

There will be times when you are meeting too many people too quickly and there is little time to make strong visual images. When this happens, look at the person whose name might be Gail . . . and instead of a six-inch Gail in the hair, just think quickly of the Gail you know as you observe a unique feature of the person's face or hair.

LAST NAMES   A similar process is used for the last name. Here, however, you will attach the object to the person's face. More specifically, you will attach the imaginary object to some feature of the face that is unique enough for you to notice it at once. This feature might be heavy eyelids, large or bushy eyebrows, flaring nostrils, a dimple, a "ski-slide" nose, a space between two teeth, a mole, a red nose, big ears, or a distinctive beard or mustache.

Let's see how this works in practice. Suppose you have just been introduced to Bill Thompson. He has full, brown hair, and you quickly see a dollar bill sticking in it to the fullest part of the hair. He has an unusual kind of mustache. This is the unique thing about him that you notice upon meeting him. You might immediately attach a miniature tom-tom to the mustache (tom-tom for Thompson). Attach it to one hair of the mustache. Try to see it dangle as he talks to you. Or you may see a Thompson you know hanging from Bill's mustache. Either way, you'll know him when you see him again.

An important point: Anything gross, weird, or emotional makes an impression on the mind. Let yourself go on this—you don't have to share your images with anyone.

How about a really tough name? Say, Sara Zaleski. Sara has bangs. Put a "Sara" you know in this Sara's hair; make her lie down and pick up a few strands of the hair in the bangs. Be sure to ask her to repeat the name to be sure you got it. Don't be concerned with the spelling at this point; only the sound of the name is important. Repeat the name to her: "Zaleski?" If I were doing it, I'd try to see a little three-inch Zsa Zsa Gabor hanging from Sara's full, lower lip. With the other hand, Zsa Zsa is holding onto a three-inch friend of mine, named Les, who is wearing 12-inch skis.

Suppose you don't know a Sara. I've found a quick way out for this. I'll mentally paint the name with big letters on the forehead with lipstick. Why lipstick? I don't know. I just seem to see it better in my imagination. You might find that something else works better for you. I'll sometimes use the lipstick method if I can't instantly do anything with the last name.

Repeat the Name

A person might introduce himself as Jim Rogers. You might simply nod your head and say, "Jim." It's a pleasant way of acknowledging the introduction. As you say this you might see a gym shoe in the hair and tie a person called Rogers or Roger on his face. A few moments later you could find an excuse to repeat the name once more with such a question as, "Jim, do you live nearby?" Or again, "Mr. Rogers, did you have any difficulty finding the place?" Sometimes I'll use the excuse that I didn't quite get the name. To do this say something like, "It's Jim Rogers, isn't it? Just wanted to be sure I had it right."

Do find ways to repeat the name. It locks it into the memory. If necessary, whisper it to yourself just after you leave the person's presence.

There you have it. That's the LASAR technique. Remember: *Look, Absorb, See, Attach, Repeat.* Put it to work for you immediately. Earlier you took a "test" using a group of pictures in which you tried to remember names and faces *without* the LASAR system. Now I'd like to have you take a similar test with another group of pictures, this time using the LASAR technique. Compare your two scores: I think you'll be pleased with the difference, and you'll be inspired to start using the LASAR system immediately.

Please study the group of pictures on page 82 of professional speakers. Associate the names with the faces, using the LASAR technique.

The "Stick-Figure" Technique

Tomorrow morning when you make your first call on a prospect, build your five-name cluster contact. Get the names from name plates on desks, from your own notes, or ask the receptionist or secretary who certain people are. Now let's assume that you won't be returning for a month. When you get back to your car, draw five stick figures on the back of your prospect card or sheet; or, if you wish, draw five circles for faces. Next, fill in the visual items, using the LASAR technique. Let's say that the manager is Sue Forsyth. First you would put the name Sue Forsyth above the circle that you are using as a face. Add her approximate age; scribble in some hair and label it blond, dark, bushy, or whatever. You might quickly draw a small figure on top of her head and label it with the word "Sue." On the tip of her nose you could hang a big number 4. In your mind you might see the big 4 sighing 4 times. Now, you drive up a month later. You turn to this prospect card and check your notations for quick review. You'll walk through the office calling each person by name.

21. Don Dible | 22. Joshua Pang | 23. Nido Qubein | 24. Don Hutson

25. Cavett Robert | 26. Lorrin Lee | 27. Ed Foreman | 28. Robert Laser

29. Ron Willingham | 30. Jayne Bremyer | 31. James Newman | 32. Dr. Charles Jarvis

33. Sam Young | 34. Frank Basile | 35. Jane Boucher | 36. Mike Frank

37. Lee Boyan | 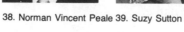 38. Norman Vincent Peale 39. Suzy Sutton | 40. Carol Gold

21.

22.

23.

24.

25.

26.

27.

28.

29.

30.

31.

32.

33.

34.

35.

36.

37.

38.

39.

40.

Do put things on those faces—like big noses—and label them. Or put a mole on the cheek of your picture if one goes there. Label it "mole" if you're not that good an artist. Of course you want to be careful not to misplace that sheet of paper anywhere on the premises.

You might be calling on 100 accounts. The stick-figure method gives you control. Without them, these names would fade from memory, even using the LASAR technique.

Believe me, this whole system is not nearly as complicated as it seems from just reading about it. Take it a step at a time and put it to work and you will be recognized as exceptional!

10

Building
Contact Clusters

Some sales lessons come hard. Once I was handling a very large account, and I was getting along great with the person who controlled the monthly advertising budget. In fact, I was even a bit cocky on how I had built the account.

One day I walked into this marketing manager's office and I could see he was in a high mood. He took a drag on his pipe and said, "Patton, sit down. Guess what? I've got a new job!" And he went on to tell me all about his new position as marketing director for a large company in another city.

I smiled and congratulated him. But behind my smile was concern—I was losing my key contact at this account. He and I had hit it off so well that I hadn't even bothered to get to know some of the other people at his company.

After congratulating him, I casually asked who would be taking his place.

"Eddie . . . you know Eddie," he said. "You and he should hit it off good." I hoped so. But it occurred to me that I hadn't paid much attention to Eddie. Mostly, it was just the usual "How're you doing?" when he came into my contact's office with a question. Never once did I even sit down and have a cup of coffee with the man.

When Eddie took over, he had his own ideas on whom he wanted to do business with. I lost a large account—and learned a valuable lesson: Always build a contact "cluster" with a number of people at every company you call on. Perhaps you will recall what I said earlier about less than half of all decision makers remaining on the same job for more than a year. It bears repeating.

Out of 1000 decision makers only 453 will be at the same job one year from today. Of course, some of your contacts will move to higher positions in the same company; this could benefit you. But a good portion of your present contacts will be lost. And you must be aware that any move by a key contact could jeopardize your business with that company.

Build a contact cluster of at least five people at every company you are calling on. There is almost always more than one person in any firm who will influence what is bought and from whom it is bought. You need *depth* at every prospect company. This cluster might include, aside from the decision maker, an assistant, other buyers, the secretary to the decision maker, the head of the purchasing department, some other department head, and a user. And don't overlook the person that the decision maker reports to.

In some types of selling, such as selling an individual invest-ment, you obviously could not go five deep in forming your cluster. But that doesn't mean that there are not other influencers. This could be a spouse, an attorney, an accountant, a business partner, a friend, or relative. These may not be easy to uncover unless they are mentioned or unless one or more of them happen to be sitting in on the presentation.

If you were calling on doctors and dentists with a product or services, there probably would not be five cluster members. There could, however, be one or two others besides the doctor who could influence the sale. This might also apply where the client firm's total employment is four or five people. The type of selling you do will have a bearing on the depth of penetration. For example, if the product or service is priced at a level where call-backs would be unprofitable, then you would make sure that your presentations were made only to the decision makers. You would not have time to cultivate an influencer besides the decision maker.

On the other hand, if you are selling a product or service that is ordered and reordered, then you certainly would want to cultivate some depth of influence. If it is a one-time, high-ticket item that you are selling, you might be making many calls, selling the various influ-encers involved. In selling homes, lots, furniture, swimming pools, or automobiles, don't overlook the children and close friends or relatives who may be present. They could be the key influencers.

When calling on firms that have 15 or more employees, and where you are likely to make multiple calls, seek out five influencers.

CULTIVATE THOSE INFLUENCERS

Influencers can make or break a sale. Get to know them; call them by name. Know their functions at work. Try to get them to talk about their work. You'll learn their problems and goals. Listen, and you will get to know their personal interests, too.

CULTIVATE THE USER OF THE PRODUCT OR SERVICE   Often the decision of which service, brand, or style is made by a user. This is particularly true in a very small company or organization. In a large company, the user may have little direct influence. However, even then the user's influence can funnel through a department head and through a buyer or purchasing agent.

When there are several "users," there will usually be one whose opinion is highly respected. Sometimes, in the course of a conversation or a plant tour, you will be able to spot who this chief influential user is; at other times, it will not be so obvious. However, you are better off having assumed that there is always such an influential user. By developing this frame of mind, you will be aware of the opportunities for "user influence" that do develop.

Just who are these users? In the industrial setting, it could be a machine operator or a technician. In an office, it could be a clerk or a typist; it could be a secretary, or someone in accounting. In data processing, it could be a programmer or a data processing manager—it could be anyone making use of a system, product, or software that you sell. With graphic supplies, it could be the artist, the photographer, or the technician. It could be a salesperson.

CULTIVATE THE INSIDER

The insider has the decision maker's ear. One clue to someone's identity as an "insider" is when he or she is called in to listen to your presentation. This could be anyone—a secretary, the controller, the salesmanager, a department head, an outside consultant, a vice president, the president, a partner, or one of the investors in the company. The insider's opinion is usually highly respected. This could be a quiet person whose influence is "behind the scenes" yet very potent in the decision-making process.

CULTIVATE THE "SCREEN"

The screen can help you see the decision maker as well as the influencers; the screen can also block your path. The function of the screen varies from company to company. In some cases, the screen's function is to guard a superior's time. A decision maker's day can be devoured by people who want to sell ideas, products, or services. The screen often tries to turn away these attention seekers. Secretaries often perform this function, but the screen may even be an assistant to the president. Your job, of course, is to be the exception— to be one of the few who do get through. To do this, you create a warm relationship with whomever is guarding the gate. While never losing your considerate manner and your concerned interest in the screen as a person, your attitude must be one which combines friendliness and professionalism with a positive expectation that you will get through. The screen will help you do this so that you can see whomever you want to see.

Many screens also have the function of actually evaluating what you are selling so that they can either recommend it to the decision maker for consideration, or so that the decision maker's time can be conserved by not being bothered with trivial or worthless propositions. Such a screen could be a secretary, office manager, head of administrative services, director of human resources, any department head, a design engineer, a facilities operation manager, a vice president, a purchasing agent, or buyer. And when you are selling to families, the screen may be one of the spouses.

In many cases, the screen will listen to your proposition but will do nothing more about it than file it for possible future reference. This might particularly be the case when the screen knows that there have been cutbacks or when the screen feels that there is no budget for what you are selling. The screen may also (rightly or wrongly) simply decide that there is no need for your product or service, or may think that the present supplier is satisfactory. The screen may also think that a change is simply not worth the trouble (the screen's trouble). Probably hundreds of thousands of hours are spent each day in giving meaningless presentations to screens.

However, it is possible for a person who functions as a screen in one area to also function as a decision maker in another area. For example, a secretary or office manager might function as a purchasing agent for office supplies, but may have to get approval from higher up for a new copier. If you were selling the copier, it would be best if you could establish the need with the higher-up decision maker, then try to tie the sale down with brand acceptance by the screen/influencer. If the first contact is with the screen, you would need to first sell yourself and then your brand. Next, you would try to get the screen to pave the way for you to make a presentation to the decision maker.

A high order of ingenuity is necessary in order to maintain a good relationship with the screen while either deftly or openly pursuing an audience with the decision maker. You've got to be honest with yourself as well. It's so easy to kid yourself that you're getting along great with a prospect, while deep inside you know that you haven't penetrated the account deeply enough to even know the prospect! Maybe you've been settling for a few friendly interviews, but you've yet to have even one interview that could result in a decision.

CULTIVATE THE "COACH"

This is a unique person who can really help you. Coaches may not be easy to spot on the first call or two, so you may not even meet one at all if your proposition requires that you make only one or two calls.

By definition, the coach is not the decision maker. He or she has been with the company for a number of years and may or may not be a direct influencer. But the coach can guide you, tell you who the influencers are, and the best way to sell them. The coach can fill you in on problems, needs, timing, what competition you're up against, and even on some of the firm's political machinations.

Why do coaches do this? If they like you, they enjoy the helpful role. Having been with the company for some time, they know the people and the business inside out. They frequently know their jobs so well that they have become a bit bored. In helping you, they find some needed stimulation. We all feel good about ourselves when we help others—coaches may get the satisfaction that in guiding you, they are also helping their company. If they like you, they will most likely approve of what you are selling. When the coach is also in a position of influence, he or she can make the close a simple matter.

How do you find coaches? Usually, they find you. That's another reason you need maximum exposure at your prospect's place of business—it's why you don't run into a coach if your proposition requires only a call or two.

If you and your contact have a cup of coffee in the company coffee bar or lunch room, you may be casually introduced to others. This may happen if you can get your prospect to show you around—

you're apt to get into conversations with others. One of them may become a coach—a friend on the inside who can help you.

How often will this happen? There is no way to measure this, but it happens frequently enough for you to be constantly aware of the possibility on every call. And the probability that it will happen increases where your services or product requires a series of call-backs. The roles of coach and influencer sometimes overlap. The coach could even be a *screen* who has taken a liking to you! A coach can be your guide right into the close.

Two cautions: A coach could also be a terrible time waster and someone who is not respected by the decision maker. In your follow-up calls, the decision maker might take note of your spending so much time with this person. Also, there are those who assume the coaching role who are negative. Perhaps they have been passed by in a promotion, or they've been sidelined by being given titles that carry no real authority. There may be other reasons why they are resentful, or even dislike the company or certain people in the company. If you discover any of these characteristics in your "coach," steer clear of him or her. This kind of person can taint your own attitude and feelings. You could even be unwittingly steered in the wrong direction. And if they are disliked by others in the company, your frequent appearance in their presence can make it difficult to gain the support of other influencers.

CULTIVATE THE DECISION MAKER

The decision maker has ego needs on two levels: the job level and the personal level. The personal level is the more important of the two. There may be a strong need for a promotion, or to win favor from superiors and admiration from peers and subordinates. Anything that enhances his status with family and friends and with business acquaintances would get the decision maker's attention.

The decision maker needs understanding; there are times when he or she feels very much alone. When everyone else goes happily home at five o'clock, the decision maker often continues with problems—meeting the payroll, competition, hoping that the last decision was a good one . . . If the decision maker respects you, you may at times help to satisfy that terrible need for understanding. You can do this through concerned listening, and you will often be rewarded for this concern with a sale.

BE SURE THAT THE NAMES OF ALL INFLUENCERS ARE RE-CORDED ON YOUR PROSPECT RECORDS   Add personal notations after each call. It's too easy to forget something a certain influencer told you two months ago. You need to record names, too, because you must be in a position to call everybody by name.

11

The Closing Process

Regardless of what you are selling or what your prospect thinks he is buying, what he is *really* buying is emotional satisfaction. And that's what *you* are really selling, not products or services. This is true whether you are selling health plans, nuts and bolts, or houses. However, to close the sale, you must build belief that the benefits you offer will satisfy. Those benefits have to be strong enough to offset the hesitancy your prospect has over parting with his money. Further, it has to *seem* logical enough to the buyer to "justify" or rationalize the purchase.

As a salesperson, you must sense the probable ego drive of the prospect; you must feel what is driving him emotionally. For example, certain anxieties may be keeping him from giving you full attention. You present the benefits in an emotionally believable manner, as you combine warmth and sincerity with convincing visuals and impressive product knowledge. Your close is packed with enough logic, facts, and testimonials for your prospect to use to rationally justify making the purchase.

You may be wondering how the purchase of nuts and bolts could have anything to do with the satisfaction of emotional cravings—but virtually every purchase does! Suppose you are the buyer for a construction firm. The firm is building a skyscraper, and you need . . . nuts and bolts. Your emotions come into play as you consider the reactions of your superior to any purchasing choice you make. Looking good to your superior means, among other things, buying at low cost. Right now you are buying from a source you believe best provides this lowcost benefit.

Now a competing nut and bolt salesperson comes in and tries to get you to switch. However, his nuts and bolts are priced higher. But at the same time, he shows you how you will get delivery each week according to your needs so that you no longer need to tie up space at the construction site as you had to with the cheaper product. You have the fleeting thought (perhaps more like a *feeling* than a thought) that your superintendent will like you for that. Now your emotions have entered the picture again. You'll also look smart to others (emotions again) because the cash outlay will be spread out. You like the assurance of this salesperson, and he seems interested in you and your problems. This makes you feel important (emotion). He points out that a number of top construction firms are using his plan. The appeal is still emotional (need to be like others), but the prospect can now justify his decision to change suppliers based on the rationalization that, since other top firms are doing it, it must be wise.

THE THREE TYPES
OF SELLING

Retail Selling
and Order Taking

A man goes to a hardware store to buy a lawn sprinkler. He is filling an emotional need in that he wants the approval of his neighbors and himself as a neat person. He may choose a sprinkler that he likes and hand it to a clerk. At this point, the clerk is involved only in order taking. However, the clerk can suggest that the customer buy a more expensive sprinkler because it does a better job, or he can persuade the customer to buy some fertilizer which is on sale. The situation presents an opportunity for some creative retail selling.

Response Selling

Someone calls you with a "unique investment program" and makes an appointment with you at your home or office. After initial pleasantries, the salesperson makes a presentation, perhaps from a desktop flipchart, an audio-visual machine, or a presentation book. The visuals are well done and calculated to hold attention as well as to build desire. However, the salesperson's presentation is virtually the same from one prospect to another: Every point in the talk and in the visual is calculated to get an emotional response . . . right into the close. The presentation is salesperson-oriented instead of prospect-oriented. The salesperson does most of the talking. It is a numbers game; out of a certain number of qualified prospects, a percentage will probably respond favorably. Based on the input of many prior presentations, a sales manager has a good reading on the probable percentage of close ratios to calls made.

Creative Selling

Let's say you're the president of a company with about 500 employees. A representative (salesperson) with a bank is discussing the possibility of changing banks and using his bank's services. This call is prospect-oriented, not salesperson-oriented. Ideally, in this kind of selling, the prospect does at least 60 percent of the talking, the salesperson only 40 percent. If the salesperson does his job properly, he will effectively draw you out regarding your present and future needs and company goals. After getting the overall facts (and only then), you will be shown how his bank would serve you well—outlining specific benefits that might justify a change.

You are thinking that it might be wise to use two banks, but you want the opinion of your controller or treasurer. So a presentation meeting is set up for a questions and answers session. This is creative selling, also known as "consultation," or consultive selling.

In all three types of selling, the outcome is still very much tied to the *attitude* of the salesperson. And in all three types of selling, super results flow most readily to the salesperson with that elusive, warm, and caring quality which is coupled with a self-confident, positive, and enthusiastic manner.

GETTING AROUND THE SCREEN TO "MR. RIGHT"

The majority of presentations today are made to persons who are "screens." Your job, in outflanking competition, is to find ways to make the presentation to "Mr. Right." Although this is not always possible, the determination to make the attempt should be with you on every call. "Mr. Screen" cannot and will not make the kind of presentation on your behalf that *you* could make to "Mr. Right." In fact, no matter what you are told, your proposal may never even be presented to "Mr. Right" at all!

This may be so because it is the screen's job to get rid of you in a nice way; he may have done his job by simply not offending you. On the other hand, it may be his job to evaluate you and your presentation, and if he determines that it is of some value to his company, presents it to Mr. Right for approval or disapproval. Caution: I strongly urge you to make contact with Mr. Right. However, if your contact is with a screen, I do not recommend going around screen without his OK. "Making an end run" will surely gain the wrath of the screen. Even if he doesn't make the final decision, he can block acceptance of your proposal. However, here are three exceptions to this warning.

When You *Should* Go Around a Screen

1. *It is the first call.* You have met neither the screen nor "Mr. Right." Try to see "Mr. Right" first. After doing so, you can see the screen and say something like, "Mr. Screen, Mr. Right tells me you do all the buying of emulsifiers. If you have a few minutes, I'd like to show you how our X-22 is cutting cleaning costs of other bottlers."
2. *The screen wants an under-the-table kickback.* I don't suggest blowing the whistle on the screen, but I see no other choice but for you to go around the screen—that is, of course, unless you are playing his game.
3. *You have been getting the runaround.* If you've made a number of calls and you are convinced that the screen has been wasting your time, you probably have nothing to lose by going right to the top. However, if you are already getting business from another division of the company, you may want to take another look at this. Would the animosity of the screen jeopardize your relations with the other division?

You may not always know that the person you are talking to is only a screen. Here are a few suggestions to help you make the determination. Somewhere in the presentation, ask, "Mr. Jones, if you do decide to work with us on this, would there be anyone else sitting in on the final decision? He might say something like, "Well, of course Jacobs, our controller, would have to OK anything with that kind of budget." The key phrase here is "sitting in." Psychologically, it does not carry the ego affront that would go with asking if someone else would be making the final decision.

Another subtle technique is to offer to mail some material, and ask "What other people might like to see copies of this?" This question may very well smoke out the name of any "protected" decision maker. You may also learn the names of certain influencers.

Almost all people who function as screens can help you. They have a tough job to do, and they deserve openness and respect from you. If they like you, they can frequently get you the hearing you need from "Mr. Right." Here are five suggestions on how to meet "Mr. Right" without hurting yourself with a screen.

HOW TO MEET MR. RIGHT

1. *Ask.* Suppose you have been told that Jacobs, the controller, would also be "sitting in." You might say something like, "If it's all right with you, when we're finished here, I'd like to go by Mr. Jacob's office and shake his hand . . . just to meet him and tell him I'm working with you on this."

2. *Try to make a group presentation.* Hopefully, "Mr. Right" will be included in a group presentation. It might at least provide you with a reason for a letter to all concerned, including "Mr. Right."

3. *Bring your own management in to make the call with you.* This provides the face-saving excuse to the screen of "My management meeting your management." This could also turn into a foursome for lunch.

4. *Go to trade shows and conventions.* Seek out the "Mr. Rights." Trade shows provide an informal type of setting that is different from the structured protocol of the client's office. Collect those business cards and follow up on them with phone calls the day you return to your desk. Don't touch the mail— get those calls out of the way first. Call each person and say something like, "Mr. Right, this is Tom Yancy with Allied. Remember, we met at your booth last Tuesday just before lunch? I've got something I'm dropping in the mail to you. . . ."
It is so important to get the impact of your name once again in the mind of the prospect . . . and then do the same thing visually, with a letter. Few salespeople bother to do this, so you will be miles ahead of the competition. Within a week after a trade show, faces and names become a fading blur in the minds of the prospects. Yours won't.

5. *Join clubs and associations.* Get active on committees and introduce yourself at the meetings. Also, such service groups as Rotary, Kiwanis, Optimists, and Lions are excellent. But don't join with the sole purpose of making business contacts—they'll spot you at once if you do. Expect that you will be watched as you give your time and effort serving on committees. If they like what they see, fellow members who are prospects may approach you and ask you to call on them.

Features, benefits, and proof make up the golden triangle upon which every successful sales presentation is built. A business manager doesn't buy an office copier because it spews out 22 copies a minute; he buys the *benefit* that this *feature* confers. This may mean that his secretary won't be away, waiting for copies, instead of attending to his phone calls. We never buy *features*; we buy what those features will *do* for us. In spite of this, most salespeople make the unfortunate mistake of loading the sales presentation with a series of features! Radio time salespeople say things like "We have the largest morning-drive audience." Wonderful! But, who *cares*? If you're trying to sell a store owner, he's concerned about meeting the month's payroll, and he's concerned about moving goods off his shelves. So this "morning-drive audience" fact must be coupled with certain benefits if you're going to grab the prospect emotionally—a benefit like "and most of those listeners form a captive audience—right in their cars—where they will hear the full message about those goods on your shelves." The store owner also benefits because these listeners are in the age and income bracket that he is seeking. Because of this, he will get a maximum return on his advertising investment. In addition to this, because of the greater number of listeners, he'll get many more new customers—customers who have never visited his store before. So it won't be just the *immediate* cash flow he'll be getting, but sustained purchasing . . . and all from these few announcements every week.

But you'll have to give the store owner proof to justify the buy: Name other firms who have used the morning-drive time for their announcements. Among these names will probably be some he admires—and you'll quote what some of them have told you about the results.

Your prospect probably won't believe you. *Count* on this; he is thinking "I don't believe him" to each one of your claims. He doesn't look like he's thinking that; in fact, he may be quite pleasant. Let's say you're trying to explain how insulation for his house can save him money on heating and cooling bills. He is likely thinking to himself, "Yeh, it *might* save a little. But what about the installation costs, the disruption, the mess involved in putting it up?"

To make your prospect believe you, you must establish proof. You establish proof with a list of customers, a demonstration, evidence from experts, and testimonial letters. You must furnish your customer with "justification information." Remember, he not only needs to be convinced himself, but he needs to justify his purchase to others. As mentioned earlier, this is one of the key reasons for swapping testimonial stories with salespeople in your company. These don't have to be earth-shattering testimonials in order to be effective.

When you hear a good testimonial, whether from one of your clients or from another salesperson, write it down to help fix it in your memory. Reread the story as few as seven times and it will be yours. You will be able to later recount the story easily. Stories that you have rehearsed will flow easily and beautifully. Be sure that they are tied to the golden triangle: features, benefits, and proof.

THE ART OF ASKING GOOD QUESTIONS

Questions do five things:

1. *Questions get the prospect involved.* Your prospect wants to talk, too. The more involved a person becomes in your presentation, the more he feels a psychological "partnership" with you. That feeling can flow right into a closing commitment.

2. *Questions create warmth toward you.* As you listen to the response, you are showing your concern and that what the prospect says is important. You "lift" your prospect by making him feel more important.

3. *Questions focus attention on your presentation.* All of us let our minds wander while other people are talking. As we listen, the mind darts off to various things, returns to the person who is talking, then goes off again. Questions focus attention and keep distractions to a minimum.

4. *Questions give you the feedback you need.* This feedback will be flowing with rich material from facial and eye expressions, gestures, and material from the words themselves. When you are targeting the company's goals and the person's anxieties and interests, you will also be getting a feeling of what drives this person, ego-wise. You're better able to tell how he feels about others in the company just by subtle inflections in his voice, and by his choice of words when answering questions about those people. This kind of feedback steers you to exactly what benefits to stress.

5. *Questions provide "partnering."* You pick up on key facts, problems, and ideas—and you can discuss these in a knowledgeable fashion. This "partnering" is very effective when you give importance to what a person has said, such as, "Like you said, Jim, cutting costs is critical . . ." Or, "From what you were saying awhile ago about your current energy costs, it may be that we can help by. . . ."

Use questions that lead into conversations. You want to draw the prospects out and get them involved. It's hard to do this with questions that just get a "yes" or a "no." Here are some examples of conversational questions:

> "How do you feel about using plastic valves in low-pressure operations?"
>
> "How are you now getting the product from the kiln to the packaging area?"
>
> "What is your feeling about the effectiveness between direct mail and newspapers?"
>
> "What people are involved in your product development?"
>
> "I read in the *Wall Street Journal* last week that a number of companies in your industry are now going to manufacturers' reps. Does this look like a trend?"
>
> "Could you tell me what you see as the biggest advantages and the biggest disadvantages in your present group plan?"

Avoid the loaded question, the personal question, the condescending question. We're talking to intelligent people. They have feelings, and they don't like questions that are threatening to their egos. Neither do they like questions that call for answers that are none of your business. The same goes for questions that are stupid, or loaded with obvious answers. Just as unwelcome are questions that show that you have little knowledge of their business. They don't have time to educate you. Here are a few questions to avoid asking:

> "If I could show you a way to save money, you'd be interested, wouldn't you?" (The prospect would be tempted to answer this one with, "No, dummy, I want to go broke.")
>
> "How old are you?" or "What does a job like yours pay?" (Personal questions and ego-threatening questions aren't appreciated by either sex.)
>
> "When are we going to get some of your business? (There are more tactful ways. The prospect will want to say to this salesperson, "Do you think we owe you something? You'll get it when you deserve it.")

And then there's the salesperson who comes on like a prosecuting attorney: "OK, I've got some questions I want to ask you. What are you producing here in this plant? What are the addresses of your different plants? Let's see, what is your annual volume? And also . . ." The prospect will want to say to this guy, "Look, idiot, go out to the lobby and get our company brochure. Study it first and then decide if your product or service can be of any benefit to us, and if so, exactly how."

We have discussed the effectiveness of a few seconds of silence during the greeting. Now let's look at other ways to use this powerful tool. There are five important points to remember in using the leverage of silence:

1. Follow a question with silence.
2. Emphasize a key statement with silence.
3. Demonstrate poise and mastery with silence.
4. Try for a close with silence.
5. Negotiate with silence.

1. *Follow a question with silence.* You do this, of course, just after you ask a question. But even after the question is answered, don't be too quick to jump in again. A little pause here frequently brings an additional answer. This second answer is usually the one you want— the *real* one. Or it provides deeper insight into the honest feelings of the prospect.

2. *Emphasize a key statement with silence.* Use a second or two of silence after your key statement of benefit. Let its impact be absorbed by the prospect. You're giving it space, the way a key headline in an ad has white space around it. Also, this gives you a few moments to feel the reaction of the prospect. Our senses of observation become very sharp when we are silent. They are dulled as we talk.

3. *Demonstrate poise and mastery with silence.* Controlled silence gives you an air of poise, intelligence, self-confidence, and power. There's no mistaking controlled silence for shyness, embarrassment, or not knowing what to say. And we are certainly not talking about indifference or self-centered aloofness. Controlled silence is simply a quiet, warm interest in the other person. You maintain good eye contact and lean forward toward the prospect. Perhaps you will nod slightly as he talks. Controlled silence also adds a bit of interest and mystery about you.

4. *Try for a close with silence.* The most powerful use of this tool is at the end of your proposal. You have stated your offer along with benefits. You make your closing statement . . . and shut up. Really shut up. Allow a long period of silence, if necessary. For example: "Jim, we can get this plan making money for you by the fifteenth. All I need from you right now is your OK." Silence. Any further babbling about benefits weakens your close. Usually, the prospect breaks the silence with a question. It might be about delivery, or whatever. He has bought. But he's telling you in the form of a question rather than giving you an outright "yes." Assume he has bought. Answer the question, but be careful not to revert to "selling chatter" about benefits.

5. *Negotiate with silence.* Silence is used with telling effect by professional negotiators. You may find it being used on you as some knowledgeable prospect gets your "best price" and just sits pondering it. This is totally unnerving to some salespeople; if the silence lasts too long, they are ready to come down on the price, make unusual concessions, or otherwise "give away the store." Understand the process, however, and you will be prepared to use this dynamic tool yourself.

HOW TO ZERO IN ON
THE PROSPECT'S VULNERABLE SPOT

The vulnerable spot, or "tension area," is that zone which encompasses the difference between what a prospect has and what he hopes for. This is where the problems and emotional needs reside—those problems and needs that we, as salespeople, try to solve or satisfy. We find them by probing with good conversational questions, by observing the person and the person's surroundings, and by using common sense and intuition.

We all have emotional wants where we are particularly vulnerable. We find a variety of reasons to justify buying something that will satisfy one of these wants. Examples are all around us: examples which demonstrate the lengths to which we humans will go to impress someone, to feel important, to get admiration, recognition by management and co-workers, status and money, to look younger, to look and feel healthy, to be loved, to feel secure, to feel needed, and to get anything that helps us to like ourselves more.

These wants vary in intensity between people and they vary from hour to hour within the same person. Our job, then, is sensing these wants and being aware of the intensity of their driving forces. We need to be able to sense the timing factor at the same time. If you are selling to a company buyer, consider these two categories of wants: personal wants and job wants.

PERSONAL WANTS   These include such things as getting a promotion, liking oneself for a job well done, self-development, and recognition from management, stockholders, and the public. These wants are intense. In fact, the decision maker can accurately measure his or her career success by the degree to which these wants are satisfied. Although the yearnings to buy are emotional, there must be strong facts that provide rationalization to justify the decision to buy.

JOB WANTS   These are wants that are imposed upon a person by his or her position in the company. They are developed in us by our perception of what others expect of us. They include wanting to stay within the budget, wanting to buy smartly, keeping inventory low but adequate, and to do what is needed to further company goals in general. Salespeople must appeal to these wants, but should be aware that there is not the same intense craving for fulfillment that there is with personal wants.

However, "job wants" can make such an impact on certain fears that they will trigger personal wants as well. Some of these fears include fear of making an error (which demonstrates poor judgment with its consequent disapproval and "loss of face"), loss of job, loss of power or status, and fear of being passed over in promotions. Thus guarantees, on-time delivery, quality, expertise, reputation, laboratory tests, and customer testimonials all help to dissolve these fears and help to justify the buy. Freedom from fear is a powerful personal want!

HOW TO BUILD BELIEF
IN YOU AND WHAT YOU SELL

In buying an item from a store, one may buy strictly on the basis of brand name, convenience, and price. But for most selling, the customer is buying you first, then the product, service, and company. Four factors contribute to your credibility: kinship, sincerity, attitude, knowledge.

Kinship

As we have seen before, prospects are more apt to feel comfortable with and to trust those people who are more like themselves. This kinship can be expressed throughout your relations with a prospect. It includes interests, past schooling, parts of the country, family, hobbies, dress and appearance, mutual acquaintances, and age. This kinship can encompass persons of the opposite sex if the other factors (hobbies, background, etc.) apply.

Sincerity

This is the salesperson's most important quality. It dissolves fears and puts the prospect at ease. It is expressed as openness and trust with another. It comes through in the face and in the voice and manner, and it is an expression of a person's inner character. Sincerity is tough to fake; people pick up on the pretense intuitively.

Attitude

It has been said that the right attitude will get you everything. When employers are asked what traits are sought most in employees, the words "good attitude" are at or near the top. In selling, it is sincere caring, consideration, going out of one's way, cheerfulness, a good sense of humor, self-confidence, good work habits, following through on details, and optimism. Your attitude shows in the way you speak, walk, sit, and dress.

Knowledge

Depth of knowledge builds credibility. *Knowledge* is knowing your line so well that most of it is on the tip of your tongue. You get to this state by reading your material seven times. Yes, seven times! That's a small price to pay for the increase in sales you will get from this practice. Do the same thing with new price sheets when they come in. A similar effort should be expended in understanding and learning your prospect's problems, and exactly what his markets are. This effort on your part translates into real benefits for your prospect, and he is sure to recognize this new depth in you. Your depth will also show as you gain in industry knowledge and in the accuracy of your understanding of your competitor's weaknesses and strengths.

Knowledge takes digging! The great majority of salespeople "get by" with a fair amount of knowledge. An exceptional salesperson will unfold information that others let slide by. It's hard work, but it makes you feel good about yourself. Knowledge makes for greater selfconfidence; it breeds trust and faith—and it shows in your sales results.

MAKE YOUR PRESENTATION INTERESTING

Load your presentation with interest. Make it fascinating! Eighty-eight percent of purchasing agents who were surveyed said that they would like to see more showmanship in selling.

Now, these purchasing agents aren't talking about showing off, dropping eggs on the desk, or similar gimmicks. What they are talking about are presentations that have interest. Most presentations are dull—they are recitations of features and more features, or they are harangues of how the salesperson's company is "the best."

Take a look at the quick pace of a television newscast, and notice the things that are done to attract and hold your attention. Your prospect is a product of the video age; he is accustomed to the fast-paced, professional approach; he expects to see events change almost by the minute. You and your presentation are in direct competition with the hundreds of fleeting thoughts, people, and distractions in his work area. To be exceptional, you must do something special and break through this "distraction barrier."

Being exceptional means using showmanship, but using it in a manner that is natural for you. I know a very successful salesman who wears a red suit, a red tie, a red shirt, a red boutonniere—even red shoes! And, of course, they call him "Red." No one ever forgets him. That wouldn't be my bag, and it probably isn't yours. But think right now what kind of showmanship you could use that would help you be remembered. And what could you use that would move a prospect nearer to the close; what would be in good taste according to what you are selling, that fit *your* standards. Here are some suggestions to help build excitement into your presentation.

Visuals

Use some visuals on *every* sales call, even if it's the tenth call on the same person. Many studies prove that visuals can double the close ratio. The visuals don't have to be fancy; writing two words on a pad is considered a visual.

If you use a brochure or a presentation book, don't expect people to read small type. Key points, type, and pictures should be simple, clear, attractive, and interesting. You should be able to read everything on your "visual" upside down. And you should know the material so well that you have time to concentrate on the prospect and his reactions.

Visuals maintain a focal point, and reduce distraction and wandering of thoughts. Make sure that your visuals can be used even if there are two or three people in the room—leave someone out and you may be sorry later. Consider this in planning what visuals you will need in your presentation. Perhaps you could carry a small easel with you in the car for just an eventuality.

Be Different

Stir the emotions. Get the reactions you want and be remembered favorably. If you're in the service business, think of ways to present the intangible visually—not just a brochure; everybody has a brochure. But it can still be quite simple. A bank in Dallas uses 8 x 10 glossies of various businesses served by the bank. Seven or eight of these are carried by the bank's representative as she calls on prospective busi-

one of the best in marketing, so I'm going to spare you some of the preliminaries I usually go into . . ."

Your observation and alertness to things about the prospect, together with the answers to your initial probing questions, give you material from which to draw. The sincere compliment "lifts" a person. Although the *insincere* "compliment" sometimes works at certain levels, it usually results in loss of respect or the prospect's not taking the salesperson seriously.

HOW TO USE VALUE ANALYSIS AND VALUE ADDED

These two terms are sometimes confused. They're important in certain types of selling, particularly industrial selling. A purchasing agent, for example, may do a value analysis between two proposed products. A *value analysis* will determine if all of the functions of the unit perform proportionately to the cost. On the consumer level, many things would fail a value analysis simply because appearance is too important. The large car that is driven 90 percent of the time with only one person in it is an example. The home with an average-sized or small bathroom, but with both a den and a living room, is another example. Value analysis is important to you as a salesperson. It's a way of making sure that your competition isn't swaying a prospect with features that sound important or glamorous, but would rarely be used. A computer sold with unneeded capacity is an example.

The *value added* concept is one that could swing the sale when you and your competitor are close in price and features. While it has little to do with functions, the concept adds value to the function of your product by adding such extras as more frequent delivery, special training, co-op advertising, warehousing goods for the customer, payment plans and financing, extra service, guarantees, unique style, reputation, discounts, and so on.

Don't pass judgment on which of these is more important; a point may not seem very important to you, but may be very important to a prospect; in fact, it may even swing the sale.

GOING FOR A COMMITMENT ON A BUYING SIGNAL

When prospects are thinking of buying from you, they may never tell you that. But they frequently want your help and assurance that they are doing the right thing. Don't overlook this opportunity; help them with the buying decision. They're telling you they're ready to buy through certain "buying signals." Here are some of the signals you will encounter, together with some suggested responses:

> The prospect, who has been leaning back, now leans forward. He faces you, and his eyes seem more animated. He may become more responsive to your questions, or ask pertinent questions of his own. He may nod in agreement as you talk. *Suggested response:* "Our delivery time is usually three to four weeks. Would that be soon enough?"
>
> The prospect studies your brochure, examines the product closely, and asks about discounts. *Suggested response:* "It's 5 percent on that quantity. Could you possibly use 300 gross, where I can do even better on the discount?"
>
> The prospect calls someone else in for an opinion. *Suggested response:* "Do you both agree that this thickness would be best for this climate?"
>
> The prospect is deep in thought, obviously pondering your proposition. *Suggested response:* "If I may, I'd like to use your phone to call the office and see if I can get an immediate specification change for you."

What happens when the prospect says, "Well, let me think about it?" You roll with the objection and come right back to the close. In the next chapter, we'll go into how to "slide into the close" after getting this and other common objections. Then in Chapter 13, we'll cover further methods to pin down the commitment.

12

Get in Step
When They Object

A recent survey demonstrated that most decision makers comment that the price is too high. Many of them don't know what the price should be, but felt that if they objected to the stated price, the salesperson would frequently give them a discount or some other concession! Another reason they give this resistance to all salespeople, regardless of the price quoted, is that they want to be sure someone else isn't getting the same item for a lower price. So you can figure that about half of the objections you get on price are not really objections at all!

There's another kind of objection you get out there that isn't a real, solid objection: It's the "tough guy" objection. Nobody wants to be a pushover; nobody wants to feel that he's a Casper Milquetoast, that he has no resistance or is easily pursuaded. So instead of saying, "I'll take it," a prospect will look at the product, touch it, and say things like, "I don't know . . . that's a lot of money. Maybe I'd better look around." Or maybe he'll get very direct and say, "Look, come off that price, and maybe we can talk." Or he ponders, then says he needs to think about it. Meanwhile, his body language may be shouting, "I really like this."

Whether the objection is real or just a smoke screen, there is one very productive way to handle it: Start using it tomorrow. If you haven't been using this technique, you will see your close ratio jump immediately. This "in-step" method doesn't work 100 percent of the time—nothing does. But I haven't found or observed anything that works better for converting an objection into a commitment to buy. Here are some suggestions for using this method.

Listen, Then Pause

You want to create a psychological oneness with the prospect who is objecting. As long as you are on the "other side," an adversary in the mind of your prospect, you will not close. You must walk with him, you must be pulling together, in step. Therefore, you must listen to the objection, even if you consider it ridiculous—and you must listen with concern and empathy. Really listen. You want to encourage your prospect to open up to you.

Live Objections Kill Sales

When is an objection still alive? It is alive as long as there is still a trace of it in the prospect's consciousness. It doesn't matter that the objection is not justified—as long as he hasn't gotten it out in the open, it will "fester" and grow, effectively blocking any opportunity for you to reach the prospect's mind. To prevent this, you must show concerned, caring listening. Even if the objection rankles you, remain calm. And take care that your concern is not just that you might lose the order; the prospect is sure to read this counterfeit concern. What you must do is to see things through the eyes of your prospect.

Agree with
the Prospect's Feelings

You can do this even when you don't agree with his logic. Perhaps you will nod a bit when he speaks. Your face must remain pleasant, regardless of the intensity of the prospect's objection.

When he seems really to have finished "unloading," don't jump in too quickly with your response. Pause. He will be convinced that you are really absorbing his objection—really thinking about it. In fact, he absolutely must be convinced that you are considering what he has told you. Reasonable people don't insist that you always agree with them; only that you listen. Your prospect will appreciate it when you show this kind of concern, and he will begin to feel in step with you.

Most salespeople appear not to be aware of the power of this "pregnant pause." For example, the prospect might say, "Your price is way too high." At this point, many would jump in with, "Not really, when you consider all the benefits you get . . . like the floor display case, and the co-op advertising—all at no extra cost." There's no "in-step" in this response.

Nodding agreement never hurt anyone. You could even lean forward—just a subtle thing, but you will seem to be drawing closer to your prospect. The quick response does exactly the opposite—it creates a barrier between you and your prospect. Your logic may be flawless; you may make complete sense. But you don't want to win an argument at the cost of a sale. You are dealing with fragile human emotions, not cold logic. You need those feelings to be right about you and about what you are selling. Even when you can't agree with some misstatement about your product, you can show friendliness, empathy, and emotional agreement.

Jump the fence so that you are on the same side as your prospect. The barrier is now behind you, not between you and your prospect. Now you're able to walk in lockstep with your prospect, right into the close. You can only do this when you truly understand how he feels!

You express this understanding, first of all, through the attentive pause. Nod your head during the pause. Then say something like, "I can understand that. If I saw that figure for the first time, I'd certainly feel the same way." Do all of this in a low-key manner.

Match the Prospect's Mood

Being "low-key" at a time like this means temporarily putting a damper on your enthusiasm. You have been friendly and have shown understanding for his objection. Nobody wants to be proven wrong. It's that old ego thing again. One of the biggest mistakes you can make here is in not allowing the prospect to save face as you show him the rightness of your proposition. Right here you can use a very subtle, but powerful, technique: *Let a third party answer the objection.*

The entire psychology involved here is letting your prospect save face while you allow somebody else to do the bragging about your product or service. You start out by explaining how another customer gave the same objection as the present prospect is giving, and tell how the customer decided to buy. Then you recite the benefits that made that customer happy. Let's see how this will work with an example:

"Your price is too high," your prospect says. (You pause, nod, and lean forward.)

"I can understand that. If I saw that figure for the first time, I'd probably feel the same way. (Another pause.) One of our customers, Mr. Smith at the Fairchild Company, said practically the same thing the first time he saw this plan. We made several calls on him, and finally he went ahead with the plan. Here's what he told us. He found that, after adopting the project, he didn't have to keep people on the payroll. By using our technicians, he didn't have the problem of paid vacations and paid insurance. He said that our people were much more knowledgeable and experienced then he had expected. In fact, Andrews, the vice president, said that although the rate for using technical help seemed high at first, he found that because of our efficiency, he was able to trim 30 percent off the cost of the projected budget of the project . . ."

"I feel we can do the same for you . . . just as we've cut costs for Culbertson, for National Communications Network, and for many others. What I'd like to do is go over your projected needs for the next six months and see how we can efficiently help meet those needs on schedule. If I get back to you with an exact cost breakdown, would that be OK?"

SIX COMMON OBJECTIONS

Now let's consider how to use the "in-step" method on some common objections.

1. "We can get a better deal from your competitor."

"You're right! Actually, I know of about three places where you can beat that price. And I don't blame you—getting the best price you can is your job. A. J. Roberts, the packer in Fort Worth, said the same thing. After careful consideration and looking at what we have, he went ahead with us. Here's what he told me: For the first time his company was able to cut its 'down-time' to less than 3 percent . . ."

2. "We don't have it in the budget."

"I can understand that. We certainly have to watch the budget at our company too. Like you, we want to be sure we're getting a good return on any dollars invested. Arnold Chemicals was concerned about this, since they had really cut some of their sales promotion budget. But they went ahead with us on a small order. They told us the replies and the actual sales that resulted meant that they were going to triple the promotion this year. Like Arnold, I believe you're going to like the immediate results. The plan I'd suggest you start with is . . ."

3. "We're using Vargo Products, and we're satisfied."

"That's a good company. (Unless you're convinced that Vargo is *not* a good company. In that event, simply nod pleasantly. Even if you dislike Vargo and hate everybody who works there, don't bristle or show any animosity.) We certainly appreciate that kind of loyalty at our company. I hope some day to enjoy that kind of loyalty with you." (Don't expect to close on the first call when you're sure the "loyalty objection" is a sincere one.)

"One of our customers, the McDonald Company, had been buying their paper from another firm for seven years—a good company. But this customer tried us for a special brochure they were getting out. They were so happy with the fine paper stock we suggested that they decided to use us as second supplier. Afton Construction is doing the same. They were with one paper house for nine years, and got caught in the last paper shortage. Because of our five mill connections in Canada, they're still using us regularly as one of two suppliers."

"We'd certainly like to work with you. (Now leave the door open for the follow-up call.) I'd like to call on you from time to time, if that's OK?"

Usually the prospect will agree to this. He might say, "Well, I don't think we'll be making any changes, but I'll be happy to see you at any time."

Follow up in about three weeks. Remind him that you realize he is working with "Vargo," but "I'm just wondering if you'll be in the office for a few minutes around 9:20 in the morning. I have something that I want to show you and get your opinion on. This "something" can be anything about your service or your product.

Consider this when you think a competitor has the business all locked up: the real truth is that all relationships between two people are always in a state of flux, either getting better or getting worse.

4. "Let me think about it."

"I can certainly understand that—it deserves careful thought. Let me ask you—in thinking about it at this point, which of these two units do you think would be best for your purposes . . . considering the view and having guests from time to time."

"Like I said, I'd like to think about it."

"I understand. Let me ask . . . in the bedrooms, with the light blue . . . If you go ahead, would your choice be light blue or very light pink?"

"I might like pink, but I'd kind of like to get my husband's ideas . . ."

"Of course! Is it possible for him to come by and look at them this evening? Let me tell you why I ask that. You seem to like this and I wouldn't want you to miss out if someone else wanted it . . ."

5. "I'm not interested."

Before you can get in step with the prospect, you will have to understand exactly what he means when he says he's not interested. You can't very well say, "I understand. I wouldn't be interested, either." What this expression frequently means is that the prospect has an objection which he hasn't given you yet. If you can smoke out this objection, you can then continue. One way would be to pause thoughtfully, then say something like "You know . . . as I see it, this will make you money. Experience with other dealers shows this has a fast turnover. It isn't as though you'd be stuck with inventory. So I'm really curious to know why you're not interested."

6. "Not now. Maybe later in the year."

This could be simple procrastination, fear of making a decision, lack of interest, or a cover for some hidden objection. It may be just a way of getting rid of you in a nice way. An unspecified future time is usually meaningless. Draw the prospect out; try to find out what is really behind the statement.

And, of course, some of the best questions you can ask are "choice" questions that give you a commitment on a point. Here are a few examples:

"Let me ask you . . . while I'm here . . . is the heavy-load feature important to you, or would the lighter one fit your needs just as well?"

"Would one of the project engineers sit in on the final decision, or would you handle that by yourself?"

"From what I've shown you, how strong are the chances of your including this in the specifications?"

DEALING WITH SMOKE-SCREEN OBJECTIONS

Smoke-screen objections are hard to handle because you're operating in the dark. Sometimes the prospect knows he's playing games with you; at other times, he may not be conscious of the psychology behind the objection he gave you.

People hide their true feelings behind words. They may have very real reasons of their own for not wanting to buy. One of these reasons is that when they say "yes," they accept responsibility. With responsibility goes the possibility of being criticized, regretful, or hurt. Again, we protect our egos. When the prospect says "no," he isn't placing his ego in jeopardy.

This fear of loss is a tremendous motivator; you need to switch it around so that it works in your favor. You have to portray the possibility that the prospect will lose by *not buying!* Show him in a subtle way that with loss of opportunity comes regret—show how the ego is enhanced by buying; that buying our product will secure the approval of others and of himself.

But you need to probe with good conversational questions in order to expose a prospect's vulnerable areas. Then show the benefits clearly, backing up your statements with proof and testimonials. You don't sell—you simply help people to buy!

Here are some typical "smoke-screen" objections you will hear. As we mentioned earlier, they get rid of most salespeople in a nice way:

> "We don't have it in the budget right now."
> "Not this time—we're overstocked right now."
> "Leave one of your brochures."
> "Let me think about it."
> "We'll sure give this some thought."

But here are some real feelings that the above smoke screens may hide:

> "How will I explain this to Chuck, from whom I usually buy?"
> "I don't think it's all that good a deal."
> "It's not worth all the paper work to set up an additional supplier."
> "Jim might give me some guff if I make a change. Why rock the boat?"
> "The boss would probably pick it apart if I bought it."
> "I'd hate to make a bad buy. Maybe I'll wait."
> "I don't like this guy . . . he irritates me."
> "The boss wants us to tighten up. Maybe I'd better pass on this."

BRINGING UP OBJECTIONS BEFORE THE PROSPECT DOES

This strategy enables you to nip objections in the bud before they have a chance to blossom and grow! The technique shows your strength, depth of knowledge, and feeling for the prospect. When you raise an objection that a prospect has had in his mind, the prospect doesn't feel he has to defend it, and he doesn't mind when you demolish the objection. Many objections are never voiced; however, that doesn't mean that they are not there. They are not only there, but if they are not aired, they may sit like a poisonous cloud in the mind of your prospect. When that happens, there's no chance for a sale.

You can pretty well get a handle on probable objections while going through your pre-call checklist on the way to your appointment. Then, of course, you have knowledge of what objections have come up on previous calls. A lot of it comes through intuitively. The more you put yourself in the prospect's position, the more you are going to "feel" the right objections. Some you can't throw on the table because they're too sensitive, or in poor taste. These are objections of fear—fear for disapproval by the boss or someone else, or fear that buying from you might cut a friend out of the business. If you suspect something like this, you can often disarm or defuse the situation through the adroit use of good testimonial stories, showing how what you have can bring the prospect approval and admiration from others. Now let's consider how you can use this technique. Study these examples:

> Mr. Smith, it would be ridiculous for me not to think that you've got a limited budget. Also, you're probably on a yearly contract rate with one of the newspapers. Yet, here I am proposing that you switch some of those dollars. I wouldn't propose that if we were not doing such a productive job for others who are under contract rates.
>
> Harold, you've probably been with your insurance agency for some time. You're doing business with an excellent company. Why then, would I think that you would even consider making a change? I guess the best way to answer that is to explain why some of our customers changed agencies of long standing, and now use us. Take Emory Lines, for example. Here's what they told us . . ."

Get stories into those answers. People like to hear stories. When you answer an objection with a story, your answer is much more interesting. So weave some real-life stories into those testimonials; fill then with human-interest details. The plot is that your customer has a problem that wasn't getting solved. Things kept getting worse. Then you come on the scene, and they bought. The customer hoped you had the answer, but didn't want to be overly optimistic. However, results delighted him. Your customer tells you the reason why he likes your company. End of story.

Analogies and "parables" are good, too. Here's an example. Let's say you're trying to knock out a competitive proposal on a computer. You feel your unit is really all a particular prospect needs. But the glamour of all those extras your competitor is proposing is getting to your prospect:

> Jim, what you're considering is an excellent piece of hardware. But so is a Patton tank. It would be like buying a tank to do errands in the neighborhood. With our rugged but small, compact unit, you'll be able to handle all of your data needs, including the options for additional terminals. And you'll have it at a fraction of the cost—releasing money for other things you may be needing.

People also object because they are confused. Your proposal must be crystal clear. It must be very simple, structured in an A,B,C style. Be careful when you explain the pricing; spell those terms out carefully and clearly.

This bears repeating: Nobody wants to look like a dummy. If they don't understand, they may not ask you to explain; they'll just put you off with an objection. They'll do this even if they are interested in your proposition. People simply fear making mistakes.

13

Getting
the Commitment

You've had some objections, and you've used the "in-step" method of third-party testimonials to influence the prospect to feel comfortable in going ahead.

Now it is "put up" time. Usually, it's hard to tell at what point in the conversation that the commitment to buy takes place. It's a kind of attitude or feeling that exists between you and the prospect. Signing papers is just a detail.

However, it is not always like this. Let's say that you've presented your proposition, but some kind of barrier remains between you and the prospect's commitment. What's happening in his mind? You must draw on certain special personal qualities in order to peg this correctly. What are these qualities?

BREAKING THE
COMMITMENT BARRIER

There are three factors in your makeup that give the psychological thrust needed to close the sale. To know them is to use them. Continuous use sharpens their force and impact.

Your Sensing Ability

Each of us has tremendous potential in this area. A great deal of selling is sensing. You accurately perceive the feelings of another. For example, study a person's lips. What are they doing? Are they drawn tight as you talk, or are they more open?

Dr. Ewin Grant of London's Chelsea College of Science and Technology says lips express emotions quite accurately, and it's difficult to disguise them. What about other clues to a person's emotions? Suppose a colleague of your prospect comes into the room. You are introduced. By the tone of voice can you tell who is the superior and who is the subordinate? And can you tell when you're getting the run around or a snow job? Can you sense why? Can you sense when a person is really very busy and when it would be better to back off and see him another time? Can you tell when a prospect is preoccupied? The more you work at sharpening your sense of awareness, the sharper it actually becomes. The more you can duplicate the feeling tone of your prospect, the more exceptional you become as a salesperson. You may want to check those body-language clusters in Chapter 7 once again.

Your Inner Drive

Some people have great sensing ability; they care and they are considerate. As important as these qualities are, something more is required to be an exceptional closer: It takes "ego drive." Ego drive is a powerful, goal-oriented force which positively pushes the exceptional closer—driving him straight to the mark. When you have this drive, you derive immense pleasure and satisfaction from making a sale. This inner drive makes you want to win and take on greater challenges.

Inner drive needn't—and shouldn't—come across as loud or pushy. It may even appear quite "laid back," and easygoing. There is no mistaking its presence, however. This drive keeps your thinking on a positive course, regardless of stalls and any negativism on the part of the prospect.

You can keep this drive alive by simply refusing to accept a prospect's "no" as a permanent answer. When you hear a negative, nod or in some manner express understanding. Bide your time and come back to benefits—again trying for the commitment. This drive will lend authority to everything you say, and give force to your recommendations. It is very difficult for a prospect to resist this kind of persistence.

Develop an Inner Toughness

You may totally captivate a prospect by your emotional appeal and possess a tremendous inner drive toward accomplishment and still fail to make a particular sale. Failures, lost sales, and setbacks happen. But with one more ingredient, *toughness*, added to the mix, you will have the courage to pick yourself up and keep going instead of moaning over what might have been and crying over your "bad breaks." You won't look any less pleasant for this inner toughness, but you will have the total capacity to withstand repeated rejections.

INSTEAD OF SELLING, HELP PEOPLE TO BUY   Consider these two questions. The first is a "selling" question, the second a "helping" question:

"If I could show you how to save 20 percent on your insurance premiums, you'd like that, wouldn't you?"

Does that sound as if the salesperson is talking down to you? It sounds that way to many people. Now look at the same information, presented in a "helping" manner.

"I've got a plan that I believe will cut 20 percent off your insurance cost. I'd like to show it to you."

EFFECTIVE CLOSING METHODS

Use these closes in words that seem natural to you; they should fit your own personality. Blend one method with another; at times you may work through a blend of three or four methods in a period of just a minute or two.

The "Choice" Close

In this close, you get commitment on a minor point, thereby implying that there has been a decision to buy:

> Would this be cash, or would you be interested in our installment plan?
> Do you believe the half-inch belting is adequate or would you sometimes be carrying loads that might require three-quarter inch?
> Do you prefer the blue shade or do you like the orange?

The Assumptive Close

Probably the most powerful of closing methods, this close assumes that the prospect is going to buy. When people get the feeling that you fully expect that they are going to buy, that very belief will frequently make them buy. And they usually *won't* buy if they pick up any manner or attitude on your part that gives them the feeling that you expect them not to buy.

You express this "assumption" that a prospect will buy both in your manner and in your dialogue. Your very posture is important. Sit forward—don't slouch. Maintain an attitude of friendly but business-like concern. Taking notes of some key facts that the prospect tells you shows this assumptive attitude—so get that pen and pad out there early. Do the same with any agreement form that you'll soon be handing the prospect for an OK. (And remember always to ask, "Would you OK this?" Never say, "Sign here" or "Would you sign this?")

Here are some examples of the kind of dialogue that helps to convey that positive, assumptive closing attitude that works such magic on your prospects:

> Now, we'll get the plants in on Saturday. You're going to see the pleasant looks on your customers' faces when they walk into your lobby Monday morning.

(The prospect hasn't said anything about buying—but neither has he said he won't buy.) You *assume* the close. You're also painting some very vivid benefit images for him. He might say something like, "What's this going to cost me?" If he does, you have made the sale! However, suppose he says, "I want to think about it." How do you get back on the track and offer him another "choice?" Try this:

> I can understand that. It deserves careful thought. But let me ask you—at this point in your thinking, do you like the idea of using the potted trees at the end of the lobby, or do you think that would be unnecessary?

Suppose he repeats that he wants to "think about it." Press gently with another question:

> I understand, but I was just wondering at this point how you felt about this.

The prospect might say something like, "Well, I think the trees at the end of the lobby add something . . ."

You answer: "I think they do, too. What do you think? One in each corner . . .?"

The prospect responds: "Probably . . . as long as they don't interfere with the office doors swinging open and shut."

Notice how this "assumptive power" builds? Watch, now, how you bring it to a climax: "Oh, no. We'll see that they don't. Now what about the ivy? What do you think about . . ."

Then put the finishing touches on the close: "How will this be billed—to the home office, or to this address?"

The Testimonial Close

In this close you are also building believability and proof. This is so important in dissolving the prospect's fear of making a mistake, of looking foolish in someone else's eyes for having made the decision to buy.

Use this close by telling a story. This is an outstanding close. Start immediately to weave it into your presentation. Here are some examples:

> After Hanover Instruments included this insulation in their control boxes, the dust and dirt fouling was drastically reduced. It cut maintenance and replacement way down. If I may, I'd like to take a look at your own units to see how we might be of help.
>
> Jason Sporting Goods added this to their ski equipment line. With this display unit in place, their sales increased by 12 percent. With your OK, I'll push this through so that you'll have delivery well before the season.
>
> I'm sure you've seen the beautiful hanging plants in the atrium of the Chemical Building. They tried to handle that with their own people, but replacement costs were exhorbitant. Now they use our lease services and we're responsible for the replacements. It helped them get premium footage rates. I'd like to do a quick layout sketch of your own lobby right now so you can see how the plants will add a touch of class.

The Hooker Close

This one gets action immediately. It's a common approach in advertising ("Buy one and get an extra one for just one cent.") The best way to use this is to sell the benefits hard, then if you have good interest, close with the "hooker." Here are some examples:

> As a special introductory offer this month only, we're including this classic globe and stand—absolutely free. How do you like it?
>
> Tell you what, you go ahead with me today, and we'll run 10 promotion announcements for you at no charge.

This week, with a 50,000-unit order, we'll pick up all delivery charges. That's in addition to the 6 percent discount. With your OK and P.O. number, I'll get this in before the deadline.

The Fear Close

We are strongly motivated by fear. We fear looking old, fat, unattractive, losing our jobs, lives, health, loved ones, power, money, prestige, or approval. Fear makes us buy exercising equipment, cosmetics, insurance, investments, computers, advertising, burglar and smoke alarms, and new product lines. Here are some examples of the fear close:

> Mr. Smith, your present supplier is certainly a good one. What I'm suggesting is to include us as an additional source. It gives you a hedge against a contingency of not being able to get the parts when you need them—in the case of a strike shutting one of us down.
>
> Jim, it's the unexpected we want to prepare for. All I need is your OK on this and you're covered . . . as of this minute.

The Justification Close

To get into this close, do a summary of all benefits—in terse, capsule form. The total impact of all of them together frequently gives the prospect a feeling of justification to go ahead. Also, you'll be covering some benefits the prospect forgot or didn't hear. Remember, people's thoughts drift. They may be looking right at you but never hear you because they're thinking of something else. This is a great close to wind up a combination of several of the other closes. Here are some examples of the justification close:

> Hank, let me go over what this centrifugal will do for you: First, it will cut your energy cost immediately. Second, you'll maintain higher pressure than you've been getting. Third, the air-cooling feature means far less maintenance. And we can take the old one off your hands and give you fair credit for it. Also, by making the changeover on a weekend, there will be no disruption on the line. If I may, I'd like to go ahead and call to see which weekend our people can come in and make the changeover.
>
> Jim, briefly, here's what your getting: coverage that will pay your wife and family $50,000 should anything happen to you. And you'll get it at a low premium that's guaranteed not to increase. You'll also be adding to your estate, credit-wise and business-wise. Also, this will provide a paid-up annuity for your retirement. You'll be building cash value that you can borrow anytime for an emergency—or for your children's education. On a cost-per-day basis it's almost ridiculously

low-priced, when you consider the benefits you're setting up. If it's OK with you, I'd like to use your phone and see when we can line you up for a quick medical check.

The Direct Close

Here you simply ask for the order! People really do expect you to ask for the order. They want your help and guidance. Here are some examples:

These are the key benefits. All I need is your OK . . . and we'll get this started by Wednesday of next week.

This ad will have impact. And with what you've got to offer at such low prices, I wouldn't go with less than a full page. Give me some copy on this, and I'll have a layout and proof here the day after tomorrow.

Mr. Jones, my company would like this job. And, personally, I'm looking forward to the possibility of working with you. Can we consider it firm?

MOVING THE PROCRASTINATOR   Remember that your client is taking a risk when he buys from you. If it is a foolish buy, it can affect his ego or cause problems or criticism from his superiors. So your client or prospect asks himself, "Why not put off the possibility?" And even if there seems to be no such risk, he may still wonder why he should make the change—maybe the change itself will cause problems. Anyhow, change usually means effort—why make the effort? Why not keep things the way they are right now? Just making the decision requires effort . . . effort that can easily be postponed. So there we have the three-headed monster of procrastination: fear, *status-quo*, effort.

REMEMBER THAT PEOPLE ARE EMOTIONAL   Our emotions tell us what we want to do. When we do something that someone else wants us to do, it is because they have made us *want* to do it—they have triggered one of our emotions. Usually, it is because they have made us feel better about taking action than if we had done nothing. You initiate this action in other people when:

1. You lift them, and give their self-esteem a boost. You do this when you give them your trust and faith, and when you pay them a sincere compliment. They don't want to break this faith or let you down. And they want that "good feeling" that you have given them to continue!
2. You touch strong fears that they will immediately lose something if they do not act now.
3. You play on the emotions of approval and recognition that they will get if they act *now*.
4. You make them feel strong and decisive by acting now. We all want to appear to others as active persons who get things done.

CLOSING THE VARIOUS "BEHAVIORAL TYPES"

Here is a quick capsule version of how to use certain closing techniques on the four behavior types covered in Chapter 4.

The Dominant, or "D" Type

Remember to keep the close right on track, right to the point with benefits, and to make a direct close for action after a quick summary, using the "justification" close. Impulsive buyers belong to this type, but expect a couple of strong objections. Answer objections directly; don't pussy-foot around.

The Expressive, or "E" type

Let "E" do a lot of the talking. Go heavy on prestigious testimonials. Take him to a top restaurant—and close. Don't be ponderous. These are very emotional people. They like to buy the latest thing. Touch their emotions with approval, recognition, money, and comfort, and you will move them to act.

The Solid, or "S" Type

"S" usually does not buy on the first call. Don't exaggerate or shade the truth in any way. Show exactly how something will work. Don't gloss over important points. What you have must show some form of security. Build friendship through integrity. Demonstrate personal and professional maturity.

The Analytical, or "A" Type

Expect this type to find a flaw in your presentation. "A" needs to know all the details and may stall while awaiting more facts before making a decision. He doesn't like pushy people and abhors mistakes, so always give him plenty of proof; show him testimonials. And be neat about everything. These people buy according to set procedures. Use low-key closing methods.

SUMMARY

The really important thing to remember about all of your closing efforts is that any "no," no matter how final it may sound, is only temporary! And the prospect never means it personally—it's just that he simply doesn't believe that the benefits mean all that much . . . at the moment. The timing of the call may be bad. Things do happen that are quite beyond your control. Your prospect may be preoccupied. At any rate, always try to leave the door open for a return call. And *do* return . . . present your case differently. Recall those statistics we mentioned earlier: 80 percent of all sales are made after the fifth call, yet 80 percent of all salespeople quit after the third call!

14

Negotiating
the Sale

Negotiating takes place only after the prospect feels he or she may do business with you. Anything else is still part of the selling process proper—that part in which you are still attempting to convince the prospect of certain benefits.

Good negotiating requires a keen sense of a person's emotional needs. It involves self-discipline, timing, imagination, a sense of humor, knowledge, planning, courage, quick thinking, and honest-to-goodness empathy. It is probably the most stimulating part of selling. If done correctly, both parties will come away feeling lifted.

In much selling, there is no negotiating at all; you simply stimulate desire, ask for the order, or nudge the prospect to action. But negotiating is compromise. It is a giving or exchanging of concessions to wrap up the sale. The thing that is given may be something concrete, or it may only be symbolic. It is the *feeling* about the concession that counts; it is this feeling that gives it value.

For example, a textile manufacturer in North Carolina wanted the contract to recarpet eight hotels belonging to a prestigious chain. Competition for the order was fierce, so they went in with a very low price. The hotel was happy with the substantial dollar savings; the manufacturer was happy because he believed that testimonials from this customer would help him secure the business of the better world-wide hotel chains. Although their profit was low on this sale they no doubt imagined the probable benefit of being known as the supplier to a top hotel chain.

For negotiations to be truly successful, both parties should feel that they have "won" something. If either party feels that someone has taken advantage of them, the agreement can fall apart. Payments may not be made on time, proper services may not be performed, and there may even be some behind-the-scenes lowering of quality.

If you want to see a really top negotiator at work, watch an automobile salesperson maneuver a deal. You may not have the highest regard for some of these salespeople, but many are absolute masters of the art of negotiating. *They* know that both parties must feel that they have won something. The first thing that they do is make room to negotiate in. And that's the reason they won't give you the bottom-line price when you walk in. If they *did* give you their bottom price right at the start, you wouldn't be able to feel you'd won, and you'd probably go elsewhere. Let's go through a car-buying scenario to see how this works in practice.

Right from the start, the salesman does his best to convince you that you're going to get a really good deal. And he doesn't look down his nose at the wreck you're planning to trade in. He reads your body language accurately. Car buying is emotionally charged for most customers, and he correctly reads these emotions as you ponder your decision. He doesn't just stand there as you gaze at a car you like; he opens the door and urges you to get inside, behind the wheel. The newness feels good, gives you a bit of an ego-lift. This shows in your eyes and in your manner.

Trying to be nonchalant, you ask the price. It's quite a bit more than you had in mind. There's a tightening of your mouth, a grimace. The salesman says maybe he can get you a good trade-in deal, and guides you back to his office, where he can "do some figuring."

You don't need to be a psychologist to see that you're now on his turf. And you are seated in *his* office, perhaps feeling committed to do business. He does some quick figuring. He has the keys to your car in his hands so that he can "get your car appraised." You wonder if he'll notice the missing radio knob, and that small dent in one of the doors. . . . You hear the salesman mumble something to the person who's going to check your car out. You get the feeling that whatever he said, it was to try to help you get the best deal possible. Your salesman is confident, warm, and relaxed as you both wait for the trade-in figure. You're anxious about the deal, and you take a couple of deep breaths and ponder over the spell of temporary insanity that moved you to come to the dealer's showroom in the first place.

Your salesman gets up and walks over to the person who

looked at your car, takes a piece of paper from him, and looks at it. Then he turns to face you. Quietly he informs you that he really pushed them to go the limit so that he could get you into a new car. More anxious minutes pass as he punches some figures into a calculator. He does this in total silence. Why does his silence make you feel so apprehensive?

He writes all the figures down on a long contract form, then he turns so that you can see the figures. Those monthly payments hit you hard. How in the dickens will you swing it? More silence. He breaks the silence.

"Look. *Maybe* I can get the sales manager to give you $400.00 more on your trade-in. If I can get him to do this, do we have a deal?" He is so convincing . . . and it sounds so reasonable that he absolutely must have your commitment *in advance* . . . *before* he approaches his sales manager. This will put some leverage in his request, he says.

You agree, of course. He leaves the room. He returns after a time lapse that seemed like hours. Was it only five minutes? The salesman smiles broadly and says triumphantly, "I got it!"

That night, as you proudly show off your new car to friends, you admit that you hadn't intended to get a top-of-the-line beauty like this but you just couldn't pass it up; it was too good a deal.

A number of strategies were at work in this negotiation. Both sides came away feeling like winners. This wasn't a spur of the moment technique of the salesman; there was some real, planned strategy involved here. You can be sure that the salesman had been observing you carefully, and adjusting his strategy according to what he observed.

Not all negotiations revolve around the price. In industry, it may be the terms, warranty, delivery, freight costs, service, parts replacement, training, co-op advertising, or adding a product feature. In advertising, it could be positioning of the ad or placement in a certain time segment, or a special promotion. In real estate, it could be anything from leaving in the drapes to owner financing. Whatever it is you negotiate, you'll come out far ahead with a planning checklist.

PREPARING FOR NEGOTIATIONS

In sales negotiating, the planning is often hazy. The buyer may have some idea of the price concession he would like to get. If a competitor of yours is possibly being considered, the negotiating plan of the competitor may be haphazard. If it is, and you plan a specific strategy, you will have a tremendous edge.

A checklist will help even if you don't have time to really plan your strategy. Let's say you make a presentation, and you're into the close. But then your prospect balks. The prospect says you've got the order—if you can make the price more attractive. In a case like this, it is the prospect, not you, who has made the first concession. He has made a concession to buy, if the price can be worked out. You are now into the negotiation stage. There now needs to be a fusion of your ability to sense the person's ego needs, and your skill in accepting or making a concession. If you have learned the following checkpoints, an awareness of them will come through and will give your thoughts and your words direction. Use the following checklist to help form your strategy.

1. What are the personal ego needs of the prospect? What are his weaknesses, his areas of emotional vulnerability?
2. What fears does he probably have? Is it fear of criticism for having made the purchase? Fear of getting in a financial bind as a result of the purchase? Or is it fear of making a mistake in judgment?
3. What are the goals of your prospect's company? What are the current problems facing management? Remember, your prospect needs to feel secure, and wants to look good in the eyes of his superiors. Will your proposition help in this regard?
4. Of all the "benefits" in your proposition, which will key in the most to these ego needs, fears, and goals? And what key benefit or concession can be held back so that you will have something to use when you sense that the right moment to "wrap it up" has come?
5. If you are making a presentation to a group, which members of the group are "strong" and which are "weak?" Do you know all of their names and titles? Who are the influencers, and what are their probable ego needs? If you have met them before, what are their probable styles? (See Chapter 4.)
6. Where will the negotiations take place? Is it possible to get your prospect off to a hotel or a restaurant, or to some other "neutral" area?
7. What is your game plan? What is your absolute bottom line? What concessions will you offer to get the business? Do you have these concessions firmly in mind, even the smallest ones? If this is a team effort, does everybody understand the plan and the role each will play? What imaginative or interesting bit of showmanship can be added?
8. What competitors are possibly being considered by your prospect? What are their strengths and weaknesses? Do you know who the competitors' salespeople are? If so, what would likely be *their* sales methods? What concessions might they offer?

HOW TO APPLY
NEGOTIATION PSYCHOLOGY

Start high, but stay within reason. You must always provide space to negotiate in. You know your absolute bottom line, but should you present that figure at once and make no concessions, the prospective buyer has no feeling of achievement—no sense of having *won*. And if you start *too* high, you run the risk of running the buyer off; he may immediately lose interest, and you won't even get a chance to negotiate. Consider the following example.

In Denver, a homeowner told the real estate agent handling his house that he should let potential buyers know that his figure was rock bottom. Three contracts came in, each bearing an offer lower than the owner's price; he turned them all down. After six months of looking for a buyer, the owner decided to raise his price to leave some negotiating room. In a short while, he sold his house.

Consider, too, the case of another Denver homeowner. This man had decided that the bottom line on his house would be $175,000. Comparable houses in the neighborhood were priced from $150,000 to $200,000. But he put the ridiculous price of $300,000 on his house in the mistaken belief that he would be leaving himself negotiating room. When prospective buyers heard his price of $300,000 from the real estate agent, they wouldn't even get out of their cars to go in the house. This owner finally wised up and dropped his "asking price" to $230,000. His house sold for $192,000.

The Flinch

Use "the flinch" to create an impression that your prospect has gone too far in his request. There are times when you must get it across to the prospect that his request is too far out of line. It may or may not *really* be out of line, but you feel that you have to put a cap on it—maybe to bring the negotiations to a close with a compromise concession. Here you enlist your understanding of the psychology of self-doubt. You need to make your prospect doubt himself here. He may already feel that his request was out of line but still hopes to get part of what he's asked for. If you consider this manipulative, you are right, but skilled negotiators—whether buyers or sellers—use this ploy on each other often. And they know quite well the nature of this psychological tool.

The *flinch* may take the form of a grimace, a frown, or a tightening of the mouth, accompanied by a bit of silence. It could be a startled look, followed by repeating the request in a tone of voice that signals disbelief. It could even be a smile, with a negative shaking of the head as though the request is considered almost amusing. You might even "laugh it off" with an "oh, sure, sure."

There may be times during negotiations when the prospect indicates that he is not satisfied with the terms. You may ask something like, "What did you have in mind?" When you hear the request, you could react with the flinch. Let's examine this story, involving Ed Williamson, a corrugated box salesman from Cleveland.

Both Ed and the buyer sensed that they were about to do business, but this buyer wasn't easy: He wanted Ed to come up with a better price. His reason (concession) was that this would probably be the beginning of large annual orders. Ed asked him what he had in mind. The figure was too low for the size of the order. Ed grimmaced, shook his head, and smiled.

"Look," he told the buyer, "I wouldn't be able to get that through. But give me something I can work with. If you can give me a purchase order covering your box needs for the next 90 days, I'll get on the phone with the boss and do my best to get your price."

Ed was using the "limited authority" ploy: He already knew exactly how far he could go. But on the phone, he argued hard for the price his prospect wanted. At one point, he turned and asked the buyer, "Can we make that 50,000 boxes?"

"50,000! That's a six-month supply," the buyer protested. "Yeah, I know," Williamson said with half a smile as he held his hand over the mouthpiece, waiting for the buyer's answer.

"Make that 50,000, but I want them imprinted for that price," the buyer responded.

Then Williamson did the flinch.

"Imprinted? Tell you what," Ed said. "I'll see if I can get the imprinting cost cut to just 12 cents per box."

"Alright, alright," the buyer agreed. "You've got it. You're tough, Ed," the buyer said.

They both came away winners.

Limited Authority

Use the "limited authority" ploy to buy time, to avoid stalemate and to keep from giving away too much. If you come across to the prospective buyer that you have full authority to make concessions, you actually weaken your own position. This is one way real estate agents help their clients. The agent can handle even an outlandish request objectively: He simply lets the prospect know that he'll take the request to his principal. Thus prideful, emotional confrontation by two egos is avoided.

If you are known to have full authority, demands may increase. You can easily be cornered with either the choice to accept or refuse. You may find yourself giving away more than you wanted to, and then having to justify it to yourself and to others. But if you have limited authority, you can put the decision off while you consult with someone higher. You can buy time if the mood or the direction of the negotiation doesn't suit you. You can convince the buyer that you are on his side of the fence—the two of you together, fighting for a concession from your boss. It provides you with options to get out of a stalemate, change locations, check out some facts, pick a better time, or even bring another party into the negotiations and start all over again if need be.

Repeat: You may or may not have full authority. But you don't want the prospect to know that you have full authority, if you do.

One of the finest salesmen I know is Bill McDaniel, a president of a large machine tool rebuilding firm in Texas. The cost of rebuilding a heavy lathe or planer could be as high as $100,000. He may deal with a foreman, a plant manager, the head of production, or the firm's president. But he always comes across as a warm, concerned sales engineer, not as the president of his own company. The word "president" isn't even on his business card. His vast knowledge, good questions, and manner give him credibility. He knows, on the spot, what it would cost to rebuild a particular machine. But he holds off the bid pending his company's experts putting a pencil to it. If there is a price-cutting request, he'll say something like, "That's awfully low. But let me take it back, along with the specifications, and see what I can come up with." Customers have the feeling he's on their side, fighting for the best deal possible. Even those who know he's president of the company aren't sure if he's reporting to someone else.

In a Stalemate,
Change Locations

In any negotiation, there should be an air of interest and anticipation. You don't want boredom and stalemate, but it can happen. Both parties have stated what they can and cannot do—you're still too far apart on price or whatever the issue is. You need to make a change . . . any change. A change of location is one of the easiest choices. It can quickly change a mood, break a deadlock, and send negotiations on to completion. Try suggesting a coffee break or going somewhere for lunch or dinner. Change rooms, if possible. Move from where you've been sitting. Suggest getting together for the next day, possibly for lunch. Do something different.

Ed Norton was on his fifth call to a mail order house in St. Louis. He was selling them an expensive computerized typesetting machine. It represented a large capital investment for the company and would also save them a great deal of money in the long run since they would not be using outside typesetting services. It came down to the final agreement: to concessions on training employees, financing, warranties, and so on. Somehow, the buyer had assumed that the software representing the typefaces was included in the quoted price. The difference represented quite a large sum of money, and the customer wasn't budgeing. Ed Norton knew that there was no way that his company could absorb the cost of the software. Within 30 minutes, the prospect's mood had soured and his interest in the deal had chilled. Ed suggested that they take a break and catch lunch early ahead of the crowd.

During lunch, Ed avoided talking about business. His prospect mentioned that he was going to watch his boy play in the semi-finals of a soccer league that evening. Ed had been a soccer coach in his home town, and also had a son who played. The two men exchanged stories about the sport and both became relaxed. Toward the end of the lunch, Ed brought the subject back to the business at hand. He apologized for not making his proposition totally clear from the start and explained how, since all of his customers had bought whatever software they needed and everybody's needs were different, he just "stupidly" failed to cover this.

The mood had changed, and there was a new bond between the two. Ed's client accepted the apology and the deal was closed on Ed's terms.

"Bracket" to Get
Price Acceptance

Sue Renfro, a sales manager for a radio station in Los Angeles, was having a problem getting a time buy approved. Ellen, a media buyer for an ad agency, shrugged her shoulders and told Sue that the client just wouldn't approve the rate. Another station, with good audience numbers, would probably get the buy.

Sue asked Ellen to do her a favor: Call the client and explain that this was actually a much lower price than it seemed. The station had scheduled 24 of the 48 announcements in peak drive-time. While it was true that these 24 announcements were not *guaranteed* to be made in peak time, there was little chance that they would be moved to a less desirable time. Had those 24 announcements actually been charged at the peak drive-time rate, it would have cost more than the entire 48-announcement package that had been presented. Sue then gave the price on what the package "should have" cost. Ellen called the client with this explanation. The sale was made. This is one form of bracketing. Sometimes this is called "economic justification."

Another form of the bracketing technique is used when the

prospect has no idea what the cost of a service is. This might be the case, for example, with a consulting fee. The consultant using this technique would break down all of the services that he or she proposes to render. The next step would be to show what these services would cost if bought separately, and then to show that the total cost of these services would come to a much *higher* figure than the one being quoted for the consulting fee package. Since the consultant's proposed fee is much lower than the composite fee to which the prospect has been "bracketed," the fee seems much more acceptable. Without the conditioning of bracketing, the consultant's fee would have seemed high, and perhaps this price barrier would have been impossible to overcome.

Concessions

Save your ace. Use it when the right time comes—the time to cap the close. Suppose you feel strongly that you are very near getting an agreement to buy. But you need something to clinch the deal. Your client, a distributor, has agreed to stock certain parts you sell—but what you want is a substantial increase of your products in his inventory. You know that he hasn't been stocking your full line, and you are certain that this has cost him business. Concessions from you have already included a better co-op advertising plan for his dealers and an immediate training program. Carrying a well-stocked full line will mean a substantially increased investment for the distributor.

The distributor ponders your proposition. Then you make the big concession: In exchange he will become the exclusive distributor in his area. Your "ace" could be furnishing display units at no charge, providing certain financing terms, letting him take over accounts previously handled on a direct-bill basis, or offering a more favorable discount.

Excite Them
with Showmanship

There are times when just the right touch of showmanship can pay off in negotiations. It can break the tension, offer relief from a tedious discussion, and perk interest and emotions. Study this case history.

An ad agency and client were negotiating with the regional outdoor advertising company rep. The discussion had come down to the number of outdoor signs that would be used in the ad program being offered. Because of budget limitations, only a quarter-showing was being considered by the agency's client, with the rest of the budget going to other media. The sign company rep was shooting for full-showing, which would demand a big chunk of the advertising budget.

Prior to the meeting, the sales rep had secured the names of everyone who would be present. There were nine people involved, so the rep had his company make up nine miniature signs. For each man present, he got a sign which pictured an attractive woman saying, "I'd cast my vote for Bill (Joe, Jack) anytime."—whatever the man's name was. He did the same thing with the women, using the picture of a handsome man, saying "I'd cast my vote for Betty (Helen)."

At just the right point in his presentation, the salesman said, "Let me show you something." Then he pulled out the signs and put each one in front of the proper person. He made very little comment about the individual signs. Everybody was getting such a big kick out of their personalized signs, that he didn't need to say anything about them. He then set up an easel and hung a large map of the city on it. He addressed the group:

"There are nine signs on the table. There will be nine signs in just this one heavily trafficked area between Crawford and Milner. There will be another nine signs in this congested area . . . another here . . . another here . . . another here. All of them will be in heavily trafficked areas for a full 30 days. That's impact! That's the kind of flash that gets results!"

He got the sale.

Cultivate
the Influencers

An engineering firm in the Northeast was considering changing its insurance agent. Three agents were vying for the business. One of them had the good sense to cultivate the influencers. On his first visit to the company's president, he also made it a point to introduce himself to the head of accounting, the treasurer, and the office manager. He secured their names ahead of time and was able to call each by name. Then he asked each one this question:

"If I should be awarded this business, what could I do to make your job easier?"

But he didn't stop here. He also got the names of the secretaries and of others in the office. (See Chapter 9 on how to use the LASAR technique for remembering names.)

During his follow-up call on the firm's president, the president told him, "Well, it seems that Mabel thinks you'll do the best job. Get in touch with her on the details so we can switch over on the first of the month."

Keep Your
Concessions on a "Bell Curve"

Try not to make the first concession. It is true that, as the seller, you may *have* to make the first concession. If you do, try to start with one that is not too important. At least it is not important to you, although it may be important to the prospect. As the slope of your concession curve goes up, the concessions become more and more important. Then it takes a downswing—concessions become less important. In the language of negotiation, you are saying that you have no more to give. Your prospect will get the message.

If you have succeeded in the "meta-language" of negotiations, dropping a surprise "ace" can be most effective. But if you continue on an accelerating up-curve, your prospect is encouraged to hold out for something better. You lose bargaining power.

In negotiations, you will want to consider the following about the other party.

The Negotiation Triangle

1. The essentials that your prospect must have from you. There is no way that these are going to be negotiated.
2. The things that the prospect would *like* to have. This will include such things as a better discount or a lower price. He will negotiate over these.
3. The throw-aways. Your prospect can be expected to try to put value on these throw-aways. And he will act like these are important concessions. They will usually be such things as giving your company "publicity" in a newsletter or other mailout. It may be free use of the company's hunting lodge, or maybe introductions to key people. Frequently it will be suggested that there is a "good chance" that you will be in on a nationwide buy "later." Think all of this over from your prospect's point of view. Then go over all three points from your side—what *must* you have, what you can negotiate, and what can you throw away . . .

Practice Negotiating
in Your Personal Life

Do it every chance you get—even in small matters. When you go to a restaurant, ask for a better table. On a plane you find that the seats in your "class" are jammed and you have work to do. Ask the flight attendant if one of the first class seats is empty so you can work. Unhappy with your hotel room? Don't just put up with it—ask for something better (at no extra charge of course). If you buy furniture and find that it requires assembling—ask to have it assembled.

With a little imagination, you will find many opportunities to sharpen your skills. Grab them.

15

How to Close on the Phone

There is a new professionalism in telephone selling: The excessively high cost of face-to-face selling has brought this about. Great numbers of prospects can be covered in an hour's time with high return on time invested.

Of key importance is the high closing ratio in telephone selling. New findings show that the level of concentration is strong on the telephone; prospects find it easier to keep focused on sales points presented by telephone. However, to achieve this high closing ratio by telephone requires certain attitudes and qualities. Eight points deserve special consideration.

1. *Discipline.* It takes a special kind of courageous self-discipline to begin each day on schedule, to maintain a good pace without constantly finding reasons to interrupt yourself, and to keep good records for follow-up calls.

2. *Confidence.* Only a salesperson with a high measure of self-confidence can handle the constant rejection and outright disinterest. This is particularly true when making cold calls.

3. *Spontaneity.* Most telephone sales talks are "canned." They lack warmth and empathy. Closing by phone means listening to the reasons for turndowns. The good phone closer has the spontaneity to express real understanding of the prospect's feelings; at the same time, he is able to get those benefits across. He is able to hear the objection, let the prospect save face, and turn the objection into a close.

4. *Drive.* The salesperson must derive immense pleasure in getting a person to buy. It takes ego drive, a strong desire to win. This is the kind of drive that can only be satisfied by reaching certain earnings goals, by recognition, by status, and by approval of peers and superiors.

5. *Quickness.* Phone closing takes a quick and agile mind, with the ability to perceive, absorb, and react to the emotions of others. It takes a high concentration level.

6. *Enthusiasm.* The telephone salesperson must enjoy talking and have the ability to present word-pictures of his product's benefits   pictures that stimulate the particular prospect he is talking to. He must appeal to the prospect's ego while presenting the rationalization needed to back up any emotional appeals. And he must maintain this enthusiasm with every call me makes.

7. *Patience.* There will be bad days—days filled with stress and anxiety. Phone selling takes a high measure of patience and tenacity, and requires a positive mental attitude at all times—a sense of humor helps!

8. *Stamina.* The truly accomplished telephone closer must have this quality; it is the one faculty that will help him bounce back from the emotional drain caused by the required intense concentration. Just coping with the restlessness that comes from sitting in one place hour after hour requires an extra portion of stamina.

Can these abilities be learned? Most of them can be. But a potentially good phone closer should probably already possess the ego-drive to excel and have a strong desire for self-expression through talking with others. The right mental attitude is critical. Fortunately, it is possible to greatly increase your native ability by programming your mind, as described earlier. Self-organization and a determination to apply the techniques in this book can make a fantastic difference. Practice is the key to success here.

HOW TO PREPARE
A WINNING PHONE PRESENTATION

Reflexes to the rescue. Once you start actually making calls you'll find that you are operating primarily by reflex, much the same as you do when playing golf, driving a car, or operating a typewriter. However, here you will be operating with words, mannerisms, and ideas. You will first need to program the right reactions into your own bio-computer—your mind. You will feel your prospect's emotions and the right words and shades of feeling will spontaneously surface. The entire conversation will flow right into the close. Nothing will happen by accident; it must first be preprogrammed by experience and practice.

Start by scripting the presentation. You're not writing a canned talk, you're programming in a structure of benefits and a process for handling objections. This procedure works like magic. Pay the initial price in effort and watch your closing ratio jump! The 10 steps of this program will work whether you sell canned food products, investments, ratchet-lever hoists, hospital X-ray equipment, casualty insurance, office furniture, fasteners, or consulting services.

THE 10-STEP
PHONE CLOSING PROGRAM

1. Steep Yourself
in Your Materials

Read all your catalogs, brochures, warranties—everything. Read them carefully. Read the company brochures seven times.

2. List Features,
Benefits, and Proof

Take a large sheet of paper and divide it into three columns: Head the first column "Features," the second "Benefits," the third "Proof." Under "Features," list all the features you can think of—a feature is a part of a product or service. The fact that your hand calculator is powered by the energy of light is a *feature*. A *benefit* provided by this *feature* is that you won't be bothered finding a replacement battery. Another *feature* would be a NOW account at a bank. The *benefit* provided by this *feature* is the interest earned on NOW checking accounts.

Each time you list a feature, think, "So what?" You can be sure that your prospect will be asking that question silently to himself. Next, write down in the "Benefit" column the answer to your "So what?" question. Using the calculator example, the benefit might be "no replacement of batteries." Now ask yourself, "So what?" about this benefit. This forces you to be more specific about benefits. The answer could be, "I'm not caught doing some figuring when the battery goes dead." "So what?" again. Answer: "That means time and money saved finding a store that carries the battery." And of course, you would add any ego appeals, such as, "And this is the latest in the state-of-the-art calculators."

The next step is to list your proof. Under the "Proof" heading, list the names of companies and individuals who have used your service or product and how they feel about the benefits you've just listed. Dig out those testimonial stories from other salespeople and from your service people. These very simple stories dissolve buyer fears. Don't skip this part—it's very important.

3. Objections, Offsetting Reasons, and Third Person

Divide another sheet into three columns. Label the first column "Objections." List six key objections—objections you are most likely to get from your prospects. Label the second column "Offsetting Reasons." Think of all the buying reasons which could possibly offset these six objections. Really dig for these. Check with your management and with other salespeople. For example, suppose a key objection is that your product is priced higher than that of six of your competitors. That's a tough objection—but what about service, satisfied customers, delivery, terms, guarantee, speed, your particular expertise and that of your company's other knowledgeable people? What about your concern and follow-up after the sale? Why do others continue to buy from you when they could get the goods cheaper elsewhere?

Label the last column "Third Person." This is where you list those third-person testimonial stories—the ones you're going to use in the "in-step" handling of objections and in closing. Pull these from the customer list on the first sheet under the "Proof" heading. If this paper work seems tedious, remember that it isn't something you have to do very often. Also, you will immediately notice a new professionalism in your talk . . . and a much higher closing ratio.

4. Write Out the Close

In your own words, write out several closing sentences. Here are some different closes for you to choose from:

THE CHOICE CLOSE   With this close, you're trying to get a commitment on a minor point. *Example:* "These come in a 15-pound weight and in a 20-pound weight. For the kind of shipping you're doing, which wrapping weight do you think would be best?" Or, "Which color do you like, the blue or the yellow?" Pick out some imaginary, but likely, prospect, then write out several "choice" questions that you can use.

THE ASSUMPTIVE CLOSE   In this close you put across the feeling that you expect the prospect will buy. In the telephone close it comes across in your voice and by painting pictures of the satisfaction your prospect will receive. *Example:* "Mr. Alfred, if we pick up your valves tomorrow, they'll be rebuilt and on your dock eight days from today . . . that's the 16th. Now, you'll notice a small seal on each one. That's the ASME seal which certifies that the valves are as good as, or better than, the original manufactured valves. And if you compare the invoice with your sheet on new valves, you'll see a 45 percent savings." Now write out three or four assumptive closes, using your product or service.

THE TESTIMONIAL CLOSE   Use this close to build credibility and to dissolve any decision-making fears which the prospect may have. Example: "The A. S. Arnold Company in Toledo had a problem maintaining inventory control in its three locations. This new software package straightened it out quickly. They're really happy with it. We can do the same for you. All I need is your OK, and you'll have it, ready to go, in just a few days. I'll call you after it arrives and go over any questions you may have about it. Of course, the full information packet with suggestions will come with the software." Again, write out several examples, using testimonials available to you.

THE FEAR CLOSE   Fear is one of the strongest of motivators. We fear loss of life, health, money, job, youth, love, approval, and opportunity.
    Example: "Mr. Thompkins, at this price, it won't be here long." Or, "A lot of people haven't had their fire insurance updated to keep pace with the increased value of their homes. And many have been *sick* about it after a fire. I can go ahead and add another $25,000 coverage this very minute." If the fear close is applicable to your proposition, write out several fear closes.

THE HOOKER CLOSE   "Buy one and get one free." "Forty percent off on all furniture purchased this month." "Sale ends Friday." These are hooker closes. Their purpose is to get action now. They're great for closing on the telephone. Again, if you have a proposition which lends itself to this close, write several for study and practice.

THE SUMMARY CLOSE   This is a quick summary of three or four benefits. Frequently the listener will not have caught all of these benefits as they were presented, or will have forgotten one or more of them. Putting them all together in a wrap-up can be very effective. *Example:* "What you'll actually be getting is 18 60-second announcements. But six of those will be done live by Tom Gerald. And he can really do a selling job. His program is tops in the age group you want to hit. Yet you won't be paying a premium rate for this; you'll be getting the special, low, 18-package rate. I'll have our copywriter work up an announcement using the copy from your newspaper ad. I can read this back to you on the phone tomorrow morning and we can go over any changes you'd like to make. We'll have it all ready to go for Tom's show next Monday morning." Once more, write out three or four of these closes. Do your best—pretend you're really selling.

5. Rough Out a Script

Write the way you talk. Make it about 10 minutes long—that's about 1000 to 2000 words. Use the material you've put on paper—the features, benefits, and testimonial stories. Include the objections, but put them in as though you're answering them in advance (see the following example). Slide from answering an objection or two right into the close. Blend and overlap several of the closes. *Example:* "Perhaps you feel you don't have it in the budget right now. I can understand that. Apex Machine said that things were tight for them, too. But they went ahead, and they're glad they did. Here's what they told us."

Use those closes you like best. End a close with something like "All I need from you is your OK and we can have this shipped out tomorrow morning."

6. Take Your 10-Minute Script and Read it *Seven Times*

Do this in front of a mirror, putting some gestures into it. Smile. Get expression in your voice. And don't stop at five repetitions; go all the way through to seven times: You are programming your subconscious mind.

7. Write a New Script

Remember to write the way you talk. Now cut the 10-minute script down to just 3 minutes, but keep in as many action and picture words as you can: such words as you, let's, guarantee, fast, quick, bite, smooth, creamy, touch, tough, feel, yank, hit, move, money, sharp, amazed, easy, simple, love, admire, grips, power, save, build, blossom, steely. Cut out unnecessary words and minor benefits.

8. Practice This in Front of the Mirror

Read the script seven times, with lots of gestures. Exaggerate the gestures.

9. Cut the Script Down to One Minute

Really "telegraph" it. Cut everything that doesn't have punch, impact, and believability. It's not easy. You're building a sales story with a greeting, a key benefit, an alternate benefit and the features and proof to back them up—a close that's assumptive, with a testimonial and a hooker.

10. Practice This in Front of the Mirror

Read the one-minute script with enthusiasm and animation. What you have done is to create a very lean, powerful, one-minute sales story. With it you'll grab interest quickly. But you've also got plenty of deptn to draw upon as interest develops and objections are raised and handled. You're well prepared . . . mentally and emotionally. From here on out it's a numbers game: Your closing-to-call ratio will immediately jump.

HOW TO SET UP
YOUR CONTROLS

You need a record of every call: You need it for follow-up information, to give you a track record, and to motivate you to improve your "score." Since you'll know the averages, it keeps you "up" when you're in the middle of a dry spell. You can easily get a readout on how you're doing when you keep a record of every call.

Your records need to be simple but efficient. One system uses a sheet or file card on every prospect. You'll need the following:

1. *Date called.* You need a date of your return call, who you talked to, the result of your phone call, what the company is now using, notes on follow-up mail, date mail was sent, what was sold, P.O. number, date of thank-you note, other follow-up.
2. *If the prospect is not interested, reason why.* You may wish to send some literature. Include a two- or three-line warm note. (This could almost be a form letter). Notation of follow-up date. "Things to do on future dates" could also be entered in your daily desk diary.
3. *Order forms should be as large as possible,* with plenty of line space for writing. Also, the information called for by the form should be arranged in the order in which you would normally ask the questions.
4. *Use a legal pad for notes.* You'll need it for information that comes in too fast to arrange it neatly on the card at the moment.

It might be a good idea to put those features, benefits, proofs, objections, and testimonial headings up where you can see them. As added self-motivation, you may wish to post the total calls made and the total sales made in your daily desk diary at the top of each page.

THE PROSPECT LIST   Always work your best prospects. Go where the money is. And remember that fewer than half of your decision makers will be on the job a year from today. A prospect list gets cold fast!

COMFORT AND APPEARANCE   You can't read people if you can't hear every voice inflection. A noisy area with distractions will cut your closing ratio. You need to be comfortable, too. And you'll need a work area large enough for writing and for catalogs, etc.

The way you sit affects your speech. Don't slouch. It interferes with your breathing and your attitude of command. The way you dress is important, too. Dress well, even if you're only going to see other people on your coffee break. When you look at yourself in the mirror, you want to feel proud of your appearance. Even though you're on the phone, looking your best does affect your closing!

HOW TO MOVE THROUGH A TELEPHONE CLOSE

The Greeting

You want your name to register, so if you're a fast talker, slow down on your name and company name. You're an important person and you want that to come through. If you speak with a smile in your voice, you won't ever sound arrogant. It's all an emotional experience to the listener. You want that emotion to be one of liking and respect for you.

You'll want your prospect to feel that you respect him as well—he needs to feel important, too. Suppose you're calling Mr. Schwartz. Say the name Schwartz out loud, right now; say it with an upward lilt. Now say it with the voice going down. Hear the difference? That very difference has a bearing on Mr. Schwartz's attitude toward you.

"How are you today?" sounds like an innocent question. But it can be a red flag to a prospect. Immediately he's thinking, "Somebody's trying to sell me something. I've got to get rid of him." You don't want any prejudiced thinking going on before you get into the key reason (benefit) for your call.

Many salespeople don't even listen to the response to "How are you" questions. I know a purchasing agent who loves to get such questions. He delights in answering, "Fine, I just had my leg amputated." He says that he often gets answers like, "Good! What I called you about is . . ."

You've Got 20 Seconds

The first 20 seconds usually makes it or breaks it. Like a good ad lib, it has to grab quickly. In those few seconds, you're trying to convey likability, respect, and ego appeal that sparks interest. After saying your name and your company's name, you show consideration with such a question as, "Mr. Schwartz, do you have a minute?" This question may also tip him off that you're selling something, but unlike the phony "How are you?" this question shows consideration for his time and helps to create a friendly feeling. Assuming that he says "Yes," or at least gives an affirmative grunt, continue by presenting a key benefit.

KEEPING YOURSELF UP AND MOTIVATED

Here are some tips that will help you to keep going, even when the going gets tough.

TAKE FREQUENT BREAKS   Spend no more than 45 minutes on the phone without a break. Then get out of your chair for 5 or 10 minutes. You could use the last 5 minutes to organize paperwork. Each 45-minute period should be considered a session or unit. When calling from cold lists, you should limit your calls to no more than 4 sessions per day to maintain maximum enthusiasm. By contrast, when you are calling regular customers or prospects you have talked to before, you may easily go to 5 or 6 sessions and still keep your enthusiasm high.

PLAN SMALL REWARDS FOR YOURSELF   These rewards needn't be much to do the trick; just a visit with someone, a personal call, a walk outside, a cigarette, or a soda.

GIVE YOURSELF A NICE SMILE   Go to the restroom and smile at yourself in the mirror, if you haven't already put a mirror on your desk. Like an athlete, you have to do a bit of self-psyching to hang on to that enthusiastic attitude.

TOTALLY AVOID NEGATIVE PEOPLE   On breaks or during lunch, keep company only with people who have a sense of humor; avoid dull, negative, complaining personalities. These people can kill your up-beat enthusiasm if their attitude rubs off on you.

REWARD YOUR GOOD MONTHS   Any time you have a good month, buy yourself something special.

STAY IN CONDITION   "Drinking to relax" can take the mental alertness off of the next day. Do something physical regularly, like playing tennis, swimming, walking, or jogging.

16

Making
a Winning Presentation
to a Group

Dick Jorgensen felt good about himself as he waited outside the administrator's office. He had worked hard to get the business of this Milwaukee hospital and had tried for three months to get this appointment. He felt that he had a good chance here since his company had wide acceptance in other hospitals. His strategy would be to get the administrator to start with a trial order of just a couple of his lines. What he didn't know was that this was going to be a group presentation.

The secretary ushered him into the administrator's office. He was startled as he faced the group crowded into the office. His contact, the hospital administrator, greeted him with a smile.

"Dick," he said, "We're just finishing up a staff meeting, so I've asked some of our people to stay and hear what you have to say." He then introduced Dick to three doctors, the head of nursing, and two technicians—he thought. But he didn't hear their names or positions clearly.

Dick felt the meeting getting off to a bad start. For one thing, he was in the middle of the group and had to turn his head back and forth in order to be able to make eye contact with each person. He had failed to get control by first suggesting that he be at an end of the room where he could face everyone at the same time. He wasn't prepared with enough hand-out material for everybody. Dick passed out the three brochures he had with him to two of the doctors and to the administrator.

A doctor asked a question about something on the brochure. Dick could tell that the others felt left out, since they didn't have brochures. A doctor interrupted Dick, addressing the group in general. "Isn't this the company that was late in delivering those hemostats a while back? Didn't we have to call them about this?"

Dick tried to assure everybody that initial troubles created by the switch to computers had been taken care of, but he couldn't shake the terrible feeling of being on the defensive throughout his presentation. Two doctors had to leave and so did a . . . was it a technician?

The administrator turned to a female member of the group. "What do you think, Ellen?" he asked. "Do we need a secondary supplier?"

"Not really," she answered. "I do like some of the items Mr. Jorgensen handles, but I think we're pretty well taken care of for now."

This woman was the key influencer in this sales situation, but Dick had failed to get her name and title in the beginning. Worse, he had directed all of his attention to the hospital's administrator and to the two doctors. In fact, she wasn't even given a brochure!

And to top it off, when Dick lit up a cigarette at the end of his "presentation," one of the group got up and stood by the door, saying, "Excuse me . . . I'm allergic to smoke."

It has been said that you never get a second chance to make a good first impression.

Expect the Unexpected

You should expect that every call you make could feasibly result in a group presentation. It might be only two or three people, but it could well end up being as many as 30. Be prepared to make a group presentation at any time and you will be able to shift from one-on-one to a group with ease and poise.

There are two kinds of group presentations: One is the kind that catches you off guard, such as the one in the Jorgensen case; the other is the prearranged presentation. While there are certain key elements that can make even the unexpected group presentation successful, *planning* makes the difference.

Let's go into the kind of planning that makes a really great group presentation. These elements aim at a *prepared* presentation, but by going through them you will see that they can help you even if you unexpectedly find yourself giving a presentation to a group.

Pros and Cons
of Group Presentation

The ability to make presentations to groups can be highly rewarding. Group presentations maximize time. You could have all the influencers as well as the final decision maker present at one meeting.

In a study made of 59 industrial firms, evidence indicated that an average of seven people influenced the sale of any product or service. Group selling helps you to contact a large number of these influencers at one time. Group presentations provide greater opportunity for you to use what showmanship skills you have to greater advantage and to utilize dramatic visuals.

However, group presentations can also deteriorate into time-consuming discussions of minor details. Sometimes petty jealousies and dissensions surface, throwing the course of the presentation off track. If the person making the presentation is dull, ponderous, and ineffectual—or if he drags the meeting out, restlessness and inattention will develop. Often, in cases like this, the final decision will be delayed.

Even if there is general agreement but without firm commitment, the interest level can plunge rapidly during the three days or so following the presentation. It's then a frustrating process trying to re-stimulate various individuals to reach a decision. Various forms of buck-passing can occur once there has been a meeting without a decision on the course of action. If the presentation was just mediocre, it may be a long time before the group gives it a second chance.

Most group presentations are, in fact, in the mediocre range. Therefore, for those who will learn certain essentials, the rewards of group selling are exceptional. Here then, is a track to run on . . . a track leading to making winning group presentations consistently.

SETTING UP
A GROUP MEETING

You may be asked to make a presentation to a group—or you may choose to ask for a group presentation. The how and to whom is a matter of strategy.

Breaking a Deadlock
with a Screen

There are times when you are locked into a screen and cannot get by him or her to see the real decision maker. You may be able to break out of this "lock" by suggesting a group presentation. This can be a real face-saver for the screen as you suggest a brief question and answer session. Or you can use this as an opportunity to bring in a specialist or someone from your company's management.

Breaking a Deadlock
with the Final Decision Maker

Here you may have interest, but you are having trouble getting commitment. You could break the impasse by suggesting a presentation to his "group." It could be that your decision maker needs the feedback from others before making a decision.

Positioning Yourself
in a Field of Competitors

If you find that you are making presentations back to back in competition with several competitors, try to position yourself at or near the end. Those judging the presentation will have forgotten much of the material from earlier presentations. And if you have been able to get close to anyone on the inside, this gives a chance to get feedback on what the competition has presented.

Do Your Homework

Before any presentation, find out who will be at the meeting. Get the correct spelling of names, be sure of titles and of job functions. Try to get some idea of what the various attendees really want—what are their interests, their goals, and their weaknesses? Strive to learn, too, what the problems and goals of the decision maker are, and what his style of leadership is. You will also want to determine what kind of competition you have and, if possible, what their strategy is.

Of course, you won't get answers to all of these questions prior to every group presentation. However, what you want is an *awareness* in you of the need to strive for these answers. Ask questions, listen, and observe. Be sure to take advantage of the help offered by those who have assumed the role of "coach."

PREPARATION FOR
A GROUP PRESENTATION

Before the Meeting

SEND A LETTER TO EACH OF THE ATTENDEES   Let each one know that you are looking forward to seeing him or her at the meeting.

STATE YOUR OBJECTIVE   So that you will have the purpose clearly in your own mind, write it out. Put your exact objectives down on paper, stating precisely what you hope to accomplish at this meeting. When you have done this, you will know exactly what action you want to take at this meeting—and what action will be needed to reach your objective.

LIMIT YOUR KEY POINTS TO THREE OR FOUR   Concentrate on these three or four points and drive them home in a simple, direct fashion. Back the benefits with facts. What testimonials can you use as proof? You want to keep the meeting crisp, sharp, and fast paced. What props or visual aids will add to your effectiveness? What hand-out material should be used? Be sure of your time limits and of the layout of the meeting room.

STUDY YOUR PROSPECT'S BUSINESS   Pick up brochures that tell about your prospect's business, or borrow written material if you have to. Read everything *seven times*. Really do this—don't just stop at five or six readings . . . *do it*! Do the same with the names of the attendees. You will be far more impressive if names are mentioned easily, you are knowledgeable about the prospect's (company's) products, and you are comfortable with terminology.

REHEARSE YOUR PRESENTATION   If you consider a presentation to be a major one, you will want to write it down (at least in rough form) and read it in front of a mirror three times. Make a tape recording of your talk and play it back between readings. Next, do the same thing in front of the mirror, but this time do it with only the barest of notes. Your notes should be nothing more than three to five key ideas in proper sequence.

USE CUE CARDS   The notes that you will actually use during a presentation should be large enough so that all you need is to glance at them to stay on the track. You should never read anything before the group except for specific figures which are important to get right. You want to maintain pupil contact with the group throughout the entire presentation.

If there are others on your team who will do some of the talking, insist that they practice in the same manner as you do (this is assuming that you are running the show).

TIMING IS IMPORTANT   Practice until you get the timing right. And if three or more people will talk, limit each speaker to four or five minutes. A rehearsal with all concerned may seem like a lot of trouble, but it's not if you expect to win.

TRY TO GET THE PERSON WITH CLOUT ON YOUR SIDE   Call this person several days in advance and explain that you'd like to spend a few minutes with him to go over the agenda. Use a bit of psychology and suggest that you want to get his "input" for the meeting. If you can get such a meeting, he will feel that he is part of your presentation. When it comes to the decision time at the end of the meeting, this leader will probably pave the way to a favorable commitment.

Get There Early

For a major presentation involving props and equipment, get there at least an hour in advance. If there are no props, a half hour might be soon enough.

Count on it: Something always needs adjusting. I have never been involved in a group presentation where everything was exactly right. You'll need to check seating for easy viewing of any visuals; distraction points such as windows, mirrors, people in hallways, or noise from adjoining rooms. Be sure that ashtrays, pads, markers, and coffee are supplied. Check air conditioning noises, room temperature, lighting, and your own materials and equipment.

You'll have time to develop a warm relationship with individual attendees. Get pupil contact with each person. Getting there early gives you time to ask questions and feel out the moods and desires of the various people.

Getting there early puts your host at ease. It also allows time for last-minute introductions, changes, or suggestions.

Getting there early gives you time to meet the unexpected attendee. There always seems to be one person who isn't on the group list. You need to know his or her job function and reason for being at the meeting.

Getting there early gives you a chance to relax. You'll have more time to pull your ideas together, to observe, and to listen.

At the Meeting

WHEN YOU'VE GOT IT, FLAUNT IT   If you're carrying equipment or material in, let people see you. Certainly you don't want to create a disturbance, but you do want to attract attention. You may pick up some extra influencers. You're putting on a show—you don't want to slip in quietly.

REMEMBER TO PROGRAM YOUR MIND   This will make a tremendous difference in your manner and your self-assurance. On the way to the meeting, pause in the parking lot for about five minutes. Sit quietly and affirm that you feel the tension oozing out of you: Your neck and shoulders are relaxed and the tension is gone from your arms, legs, fingers, and toes. Then affirm aloud, "We're going to have a good meeting. I like these people, and we're going to get along great." When you get to the meeting site, look at the room and the fixtures, the chairs, tables, etc. Say to yourself, "I will find ways to help every person who is going to be in this room."

EXPECT A LITTLE ANXIETY   There is nothing wrong with a little anxiety—it's really quite normal, and it keeps you alert. However, when anxiety gets too high, tension develops. If you feel this happening to you, duck out to the restroom before the meeting. Face the mirror and give it a big smile. Take three deep breaths and affirm, "I like these people and we'll get along great." You'll be able to walk out of the restroom with an easy warmth, poise, and confidence.

YOU HAVE TWENTY SECONDS   Twenty seconds is about all you have to make a good impression. During this time you are being judged for poise, warmth, confidence, and sincerity. That doesn't sound like much time, but it's really just a matter of your having the right attitude about the meeting—it's a matter of your *knowing* that you have it. If someone introduces you to the group, smile and thank him as you face the group. Pause before beginning to speak. Be natural. You may wish to open with a key benefit to get attention. Here's an example:

"I have an idea to present to you this morning which I believe will markedly reduce your packaging costs. But before I get into the method, I want to say that I've been looking forward to this meeting . . . and to the chance it has given me to meet and talk with each of you."

Take the time to make pupil contact with as many people as you can. Don't rush it.

If you plan to tell a joke, expect it to flop. It may not, but if you are prepared for only a mediocre reaction, it won't shake your confidence if it bombs. It will *probably* bomb, but by preparing for this, you'll just shrug it off without embarrassment. Your audience will appreciate your self-assurance.

USE HUMOR THAT COMES NATURALLY   Some of the best humor is a short "put-down" of yourself. It can be a very quick story or maybe a remark about your bald head (or whatever)—anything that shows you're human. I inject some humor when I'm talking to a group of salespeople. I explain that it takes two things to make it in selling. Then I write the word "GUTS" on a flip chart. Next, I say it takes brains, and I write BR——, and pause as though I'm not sure that an "A" comes next. It usually brings a good laugh.

IF IT MIGHT OFFEND, LEAVE IT OUT   I once worked for a company that gave me the honor of addressing some 60 of the company's dealers at a breakfast meeting. All of my company's salespeople were there, and I was going to show them how to make a good group presentation. I had the perfect opening joke—an Aggie joke. "Aggie" jokes are put-down jokes that people in Texas tell about students of Texas A&M. The jokes portray these students as being idiotic, and although they are meant as a good-natured spoof, some old time A&M alumni don't appreciate the jokes at all. I had forgotten that our best dealer (who was in the audience) was a proud Aggie.

I got halfway through the joke when this gentleman stood up. His face was red. He said, "Mr. Patton, I didn't come to this breakfast to be insulted." A hush came over the audience. I stumbled through my presentation.

This dealer was our best customer. He stopped doing business with my firm and completely refused to see me.

It took another salesman's efforts to get the business back. He had to apologize for me, and explained that Patton meant well, but just didn't know much about telling jokes.

KEEP YOUR VISUALS LARGE, CLEAR, AND SIMPLE   The same goes for your speech. Use short sentences with action words that create pictures in the mind. Talk to the group, not to something on the flip-chart or the projection screen. As you make your presentation, be sure that your eye contact includes each member of the group. Address people by name, and don't direct more attention to Mr. Right than to anyone else. You must make everybody in the group feel important.

YOU'RE DEALING WITH AN EIGHT-MINUTE ATTENTION SPAN   Holding attention is a constant battle. Divide the presentation so that you are doing something different every eight minutes. Plan this in advance. It needn't be dramatic—the "something different" may be simply that you get up from the table after eight minutes and write something on your flipchart. If you are talking to a very large group, you might walk down the aisle after eight minutes and pass something out. Questions, or any kind of input from the group, can serve as an "eight-minute" break. These breaks have the effect of renewing the attention span. Each time you break in this way, you have the group's attention for another eight minutes.

AVOID PROLONGED DISSERTATIONS   Prolonged speeches delivered from behind a lectern are boring—avoid them. Move around; keep the show interesting. Remember, we're competing with the video culture. Things move and change on video. Notice the moment-by-moment changes, the different camera angles on television. These changes are all carefully planned to hold your attention.

BE AWARE OF WHAT YOUR AUDIENCE IS DOING   Anyone who is doodling is not listening. If you see anybody squirming—even slightly—change something immediately. Squirming is a sign of boredom and restlessness.

SLIDE SHOWS SHOULD HAVE EIGHT-MINUTE BREAKS, TOO   If you're putting on a slide presentation, find a place to break after about eight minutes. Turn the lights on and make some comments or encourage audience participation through a question and answer session. Long slide presentations can lull a prospect into a stupor. Also, you lose eye contact in the darkness. This is one advantage of an overhead projector; you needn't darken the room and can thus maintain good eye contact with your listeners.

ALWAYS HAVE SOMETHING TO HAND OUT   It may be no more than a printed agenda or a list of key benefits. Keep in mind, however, that if you pass anything out during the presentation, the participants may be reading instead of listening. A good way to avoid this is to have your material in place well ahead of starting time, or to have it available after the meeting.

BRINGING UP OBJECTIONS YOURSELF   You build credibility by bringing up objections and answering them. If someone in the group brings up an objection, be sure to answer it by using the "In Step" method described in Chapter 12. You may get an objection that is simply a method to let the objector show off his knowledge. Remember, nobody wants to be proven wrong in front of a group. This is one good reason for anticipating these objections and answering them yourself.

GROUP SELLING REQUIRES GROUP PARTICIPATION   Invite questions and answer them—just remember to keep control, to stay in charge. Stop any cross-haggling between participants by interrupting in a pleasant manner.

MAKE A STRONG SUMMARY CLOSE   Sometimes, if you wait until the end before asking "Any questions?" there will be a lull—a deadly silence that can be anticlimactic to an otherwise good presentation. To avoid this possibility, try something like this: "Folks, I certainly appreciate the opportunity you have given me. Before I summarize what I believe will be a very profitable program for you, I'd like to answer any questions you may have." If there are no questions after a reasonable pause, go into your summary close. Label each point first, second, third.

If your objective is to close the sale at this time, ask for the business. For instance, you might say, "All I need is your ok, and we'll get this started the first of the month."

AFTER YOU'VE ASKED FOR THE BUSINESS, WAIT FOR AN ANSWER   You've said all you need to say and you've asked for action. Now, shut up. Wait for a response. Just stand still or sit still and wait. This is where somebody with clout may speak up and say, "I like it. What do the rest of you think? It is for this moment that you tried to review your agenda with "Mr. Right" a few days earlier. Psychologically, you have made him a part of your presentation.

FOLLOWING UP   Write a short letter to everyone participating (unless, of course, it's a very large group). Be sure that you have all the names spelled correctly. A simple note like the following will do the trick:

> It was certainly good meeting you yesterday. I'll be getting the detailed plans to Mr. Sloan as he suggested. I look forward to working with you and your people. Should any questions come up, I hope you'll give me a call at my office.

CALL YOUR HOST   The last step in your follow-up program is to call Mr. Right the following day. Thank him for having given you the opportunity to make the presentation. And remember to follow through with any reports, facts, or finalized figures needed.

17
Programming Your Mind for Achievement

We have come full cycle ... from using psychology on yourself in "Bold Is Beautiful" through various techniques and psychological strategies to effectively close sales. Now we're back to self-psychology ... with a specific method to actually program your brain to exceptional achievement starting right now. The method is realistic. It works.

Each of us came into this world equipped with a powerful "biocomputer." From the very beginning, this computer was being programmed by the circumstances of our lives, our contacts with others, and by things we did and said. By the time we were six or seven years old, this computer was fairly well programmed so that we could perform important life functions such as walking, talking, and behaving in a "civilized" manner in public—and we could perform these functions with little or no conscious thought.

Most people can accept that this kind of programming has occurred. What is harder to fully comprehend, or believe, is that the programming is still going on. But—and here is the important point—not only is it "going on" in you and in me right now, but *we are doing much of the programming ourselves*! You and I are programming our own biocomputers every day without even being aware that we are doing it.

People sometimes ask if "mind programming" really works. To

me the question is not whether it works, but whether you will do the programming consciously, putting in those things you want to be there. Or will you let "life's circumstances" do the whole job for you?

But let's not kid ourselves about how this works or what we can actually do with it. Let's use the comparison of programming a man-made computer and programming our own computer brain. A man-made computer comes with a CPU (central processing unit), a ROM (read only memory), and an RAM (random access memory). These are fixed abilities and capacities of the computer. The limitations vary with different kinds and sizes of computers.

Similarly, we were born with certain capacities and limitations. All the believing and positive thinking in the world is not going to get us off the ground by flapping our arms up and down: It is a physical limitation built into us. But we have a fantastic computer brain that can take a belief and positive thinking to guide us into aerodynamics and the invention of the airplane. Like the man-made computer, "capacities" vary between human computers. Those with great capacities in certain areas you might call "talents" or "leanings." Thus one person could compose beautiful music but have difficulty with the theory of relativity.

Each one of us has many gifted "leanings," or great capacities—talents that we may explore only moderately. Here again we can make the comparison to man-made computers. Many people buy computers but actually tap only a small fraction of their computer's capacity. What about our brain computer? Scientists have estimated that most of us utilize less than one-tenth of our brain's capacity.

We sense our individual leanings or talents through subtle recurring desires and interests. But too often we let life's circumstances, other people, and ourselves "punch the wrong keys" of our brain computer. We program in doubt and fear—and block out those "leanings" that are trying to come through.

Let's check your own leanings or talents. Since you have read this far, you definitely have great capacities—"leanings"—in working with people, in being exceptional, in the ability to make money, and to influence others. If you did not have this great capacity in your makeup, your interest would not have carried you to this point. This interest shows that the great "capacity" is certainly there. That doesn't mean you don't have other leanings or talents—we all have. And we take many of them for granted. Many we never even tap or develop.

Let's take this great "capacity" that you have right now and show, step by step, how you will program it to exceptional achievement in closing sales. From my experience it is a five-step process, although the steps seem to blend into one another. I would never speak so insistently for this kind of mind programming if it hadn't already worked in my life. And I certainly had some skepticism of the measured effectiveness of mind programming. I know, now, that it works. But I have also found that results build gradually. You can program into your mind certain things such as making an excellent presentation and expect and receive a warm reception two hours later. However, for such things as programming a very large income, you must maintain daily "mind conditioning" and certainly expect and receive results . . . but not instantly. You can't expect to play the "Moonlight Sonata" the day after learning the piano keyboard.

THE KEY TO
MIND PROGRAMMING

The secret to achieving results through mind programming is the ability to "sell" or "condition" the *subconscious* mind, not the conscious mind. It can be discouraging when we get all hyped up to some kind of positive thinking method and then get no results. What happens is that the subconscious mind simply doesn't believe it. For example, you may wish to have a high annual income and you decide to think positively that it is yours. You even visualize it in your mind quite frequently, even picture the things it will buy. You get no results. You end up thinking that a positive mental attitude in life is certainly a good thing, but as far as programming your mind to reaching a certain income level, and having it happen . . . well, you have your doubts. You're a bit disillusioned.

The problem was that your conscious mind was sold on the idea but your subconscious wasn't. Your subconscious didn't accept the idea. We are all locked into a "comfort" zone as far as our subconscious minds are concerned. It is the area in which your own subconscious believes you "belong" in the amount of income you earn, your abilities, even your social or business status. This zone has upper and lower "barriers." When we push against the upper "barrier," certain fears and self-doubts occur.

Studies have been made of commissioned sales people who suddenly experience a large commission. Most will relax their efforts or do what it takes to get back to where their subconscious believes they belong. It happens to athletes who suddenly get ahead of an opponent. It's the reason for the expression "He couldn't stand prosperity." The barriers on your comfort zone have been set by all the "input" of life's circumstances since you were an infant. The positive and the negative inputs have determined our subconscious self-image.

So, to program you mind to exceptional achievement, you must raise that top barrier in the subconscious. You must actually "sell" the subconscious that a new, much higher barrier exists. First, step into this with an open mind. Temporarily suspend doubts or disbelief. It requires an investment of only five minutes a day. Don't evaluate it or pass judgment on its effectiveness for at least 30 days. Second, give that five minutes of daily mind programming *top priority*. You are literally programming your life; it must be the most important thing you will do each day. And it must be consistent—it must happen *every day*. Third, be alone when you do your mind programming; you do not want distractions or any feelings of self-consciousness in front of others. I'll discuss the physical and mental method of exactly how to put yourself into a "conditioned state" for programming your mind. Before I do that, let's go through five essentials.

THE FIVE STEPS OF EFFECTIVE MIND PROGRAMMING

Step One

You must have *Desire*. You must really want to achieve what you are going to program. It cannot be someone else's desire. In persuading people to buy your ideas, you really *desire* to be outstanding and exceptional. You don't just wish you had a much larger annual income, you *emotionally* desire it. People who have created wealth may or may not have been conscious of these steps in mind programming, but they were going through them. And, of course, this does not apply to just wealth. A person's burning desire may be a doctorate in science or to paint landscapes.

Step Two

You "feel" the end result. You actually see yourself having accomplished what you are programming. Don't be concerned if this seems difficult at first. But don't sidestep it, either. Picture the checks coming in or the car or house you want. Picture your own management's pride in you . . . possibly smiling or shaking hands with you. "Feel" yourself confident, relaxed, and very effective as you close a sale. This kind of picturing with people or getting a contract signed may not be as clear in your imagination as such things as a car. It's hard to picture a prospect you haven't even met—it's quite nebulous. But just make it as clear as you can. Try to actually "feel" the event in your imagination.

Step Three

You must have *method*. Here is where I take exception to some of the "rah-rah" boys of positive thinking that lead you to think that all you need to do is *believe* and to *visualize* and the goal will be yours. You may consciously desire a very high income . . . and tell yourself that you believe it will be yours—even visualize the money. But your subconscious isn't sold. That "barrier" is just where it was. Yes, you must believe and visualize, but to sell your subconscious mind, you absolutely must have a *method of achievement*.

Now, the final method of achievement may end up being completely different. In fact, you can *expect* changes—even interesting and delightful developments that may change the route of achievement. Here are some examples of method in being exceptional in closing sales. The very reading of this book is part of method. You are seeing how you will "read" people better, go boldly for larger orders, use the "in-step" method of handling objections, and so on. Method is planning which customers to see about increasing their business—listing top-priority prospects, getting prior information about them on the phone, deciding what visuals and testimonials to use with each, following through on a set number of follow-up calls . . .

Method is taking that annual income figure you really want and dividing it by 2,000—that's the number of working hours in a year and it pinpoints what your hourly "rate" is. It makes you far more aware of time management and planning, and practically shows you how much closing you're going to have to accomplish day to day or week to week. It may lead you to go for larger sales, or top of the line, or selling the full line. Add method and you "convince" your subconscious mind.

Step Four

You must take some *action* on any goal every day. This can be as little as 10 minutes a day, but it must be *every* day. It may be being alone and mapping out a closing strategy; it may be thinking through and visualizing a closing process with a large prospect; it may be reading material about that prospect's business.

Step Five

You must expect to *fall on your face* on the way to your achievement. This may happen a number of times. Simply get up and keep going. In the records of people's achievements that I have studied, large and small, I have yet to find an achievement where there were not setbacks along the way.

This fact is all-important to you—it is why most people never achieve what that want in life: At the first setback or two, they become discouraged. Or some well-meaning person says, "I told you so . . . I told you that you'd never sell that company." There are lots of "I told you so" people in this world. They never made it that big in their own lives, but they don't hesitate to tell you how to run yours. Ignore the "I told you so" people. You can book it: You are going to fall on your face on the way. This is not negative thinking—it is realistic, positive thinking. Now that you know, now that you are prepared, it won't hurt. You'll just keep going . . . in spite of what people think and say.

THE METHOD OF PUTTING YOURSELF INTO A "CONDITIONED" STATE OF MIND

Call it self-hypnosis, altered-state, brain-washing, or "conditioned" state of mind: We've been doing this to ourselves all our lives in various ways. What we're going to do here is use a conscious, planned method of *programming what we want* in order to *achieve what we want.*

1. *Be alone.* Sit in a chair or a car. Allow yourself at least five minutes. You will need several minutes to get into the state where you are programming directly to your subconscious mind. Do not expect anything unusual. Your conditioned state will be much the same when you awake in the morning—not fully conscious, but aware of your own thoughts. Or it may be very much like the very relaxed state just before going to sleep. Get comfortable, but not so comfortable that you'll fall off into a sleep. However, do not be concerned if you do fall asleep from time to time.

2. Fix your gaze on a spot on the wall or a leaf. Concentrate on that one spot. You are going to put yourself in a very deep, conditioned state. As you stare at the spot, tell yourself aloud: "I am now going to relax deeply. I am now going to program my mind and my life."

3. As you try to stare at the spot, tell yourself, "All the tension is running out of my body . . . all the tension is leaving the neck, the arms . . . it's all running out my fingertips (try to feel this leaving the fingers). Now all the tension is going out of the body . . . out of the legs . . . and flowing right out the toes (try to feel the tension leaving the toes). I am now in a deep, deep, relaxed state."

4. As you continue to stare at the spot, tell yourself, "My eyelids are getting very heavy . . . I cannot keep them from closing." At this point even if you try to hold your eyes open, they will probably close. You are in contact with your subconscious. If they do not close, do not

be concerned. Simply continue with, "I'm going deeper, deeper, deeper . . . I am very relaxed . . . very, very relaxed." Then try to see yourself descending on a very long escalator. Do this as though you are seeing yourself descend . . . you see yourself getting smaller and smaller as you watch yourself slowly descend the long, long escalator. If your eyes still have not closed, go through the tension release of the body (out the fingers and out the toes).

5.　Your eyes will close. You are now ready to program your mind. But wait just a bit. Thoughts will start flowing in; patiently "sweep" them out. Don't encourage them; instead, try not to think of anything in particular. You will experience what I call "sub-thoughts"—a sort of awareness that you're thinking, but thinking of nothing in particular.

6.　Now program in your affirmations. These must always be positive. For example, "Today I am very confident," not "Today I won't be nervous." Say the affirmation out loud. Hold it to a few—not over five—affirmations. Three would be ideal. These are things you really want. After each affirmation, say these words: "I accept this. It is now programmed."

7.　Here are some suggested affirmations for exceptional achievement in closing sales and some "picturing" you might use. Of course, you can use such programming for any achievements in life.

"Today I am bold, very confident, carefree, and happy. I accept this; it is now programmed." "Feel" yourself walking upright, happy, saying "hello" to people, smiling, and feeling good.

"Today I shall make great presentations. I will have warmth with everyone I meet. I close sales easily. I accept this; it is now programmed." "Feel" yourself with a new customer, smiling at each other as he takes your pen to sign the order.

"Today I have great self-discipline. I get things done quickly. I do first things first. I have the guts to say no to the things I don't want to do or shouldn't do. I accept this; it is now programmed." See yourself crossing out the "A" items on your "to do" list. Visualize your orderly desk as you concentrate on writing a presentation.

"Today I shall remember names easily. I accept this; it is now programmed." You might "feel" yourself walking through a prospect's office, confidently, looking and greeting each person by name as you pass by various desks and offices.

"I shall earn $_____ a year." (Make this an exact goal figure that you really want and can accept as possible after planning "Method" in Step Three. "Today I am doing all the right things that earn $_____ a year. I accept this; it is now programmed." Picture the figure clearly on a sheet of paper and picture your hourly "rate." See certain amounts on your paychecks. See yourself amongst others making similar incomes. "Feel" some end result—a new home or figure in a savings account.

"Today I have fantastic energy. I have great stamina and enthusiasm all day today. I accept this; it is now programmed." "Feel" yourself running and jumping or running up stairs or swinging on the overhead bars. "Feel" yourself walking fast, head up, smiling, loving life and people.

8.   When you complete the programming, your eyes will open. And I believe you will notice that you feel quite refreshed.

Again, do not try to program too many goals into your mind at once. Choose only those you *really* want expressed in your life. Stay with them on a daily basis. As one is expressed in your life, you may choose to substitute it for another. Some you may never change. I find I must program the one on discipline and the affirmation on energy continuously.

Give this system a good trial. Stay with the method at least 30 days before you pass judgment on its effectiveness. Aside from reaching certain goals, you'll get a great release from daily tension and stress. Be sure you are making the programming session the most important five minutes of your day. Do not be casual about this fact—and expect the changes to be gradual.

To accomplish major goals, don't underestimate the value of a *written plan*. In a study of Harvard alumni who had been out of school for 10 years, the 3 percent of graduates who had written plans earned 10 times as much as the 83 percent who had neither mental nor written plans. If there is magic in the world, it is surely in what we can do with ourselves when we strike off the shackles of fear and self-doubt. Besides, it's more *fun* to be exceptional!

Take this book and its method and run with it. Begin at once to program your mind and let the techniques and procedures in these chapters take hold. You'll outflank your competition. You'll leap ahead in income. If there is a shortcut to very high income, I am convinced that it is in making yourself a powerful closer—and you have the method to accomplish this goal in your hands, right now. All you need is the commitment to turn on your own truly magical power.

Let that boldness within you flow! Once more, feel the impact of these lines from Goethe:

WHATEVER YOU CAN DO, OR DREAM YOU CAN, BEGIN IT! BOLDNESS HAS GENIUS, POWER AND MAGIC IN IT.

Index